"Jordan Morrow has done it again. This flows on perfectly from his first book, *Be Data Literate*, and creates a realistic and achievable pathway for organizations to become data driven. And, of course, at the center of it is people—a man after my own data heart! I hope that wasn't a spoiler alert…"

Susan Walsh, The Classification Guru and author of *Between the Spreadsheets*

"Understanding the basics of data science and AI is key to succeeding today. This book provides key insights into preparing better for a more data-driven future. A fascinating read for anyone looking to stay on top of how data science is revolutionizing just about everything. Jordan Morrow has done an amazing job taking a complex topic and synthesizing it for all to understand. Highly recommended."

Manuj Aggarwal, Founder and Chief Innovation Officer, TetraNoodle

"Jordan Morrow delivers a great follow-up to his first book, *Be Data Literate*. With this new book, he helps us understand what being data driven actually means and why it matters. He then offers a simple, practical approach to help companies get there. For organizations and leaders who know there is value in their data but have struggled to unleash it, this is the book for you."

Brian Ferris, Chief Data, Analytics and Technology Officer, Loyalty NZ

"One of the pioneers in the field of data."

Jimmy Rex, investor, author and podcast host of *The Jimmy Rex Show*

"Jordan Morrow is a true authority on data literacy and the opportunity for organizations that want to become data driven. In this book, he covers all the critical ingredients organizations need to become truly data driven in a world that's been transformed by the

Covid-19 pandemic. His second book is a great guide for leaders and practitioners alike and provides the necessary tools for transforming your business into a data-driven powerhouse."
Eva Murray, Lead Evangelist EMEA, Snowflake

"Jordan Morrow has followed his brilliant first book, *Be Data Literate*, with this masterpiece. It's a comprehensive and insightful book in which he shares his passion and experience in the data space to give everyone the power to harness the true power of data."
Bernard Marr, best-selling author, futurist, business and technology adviser

"This book aims high, with strong data culture principles and data literacy foundations, while maintaining significant focus on the strategy that guides data initiatives to successful completion and mission success. Failure is not an option in this data-intensive world. *Be Data Driven* is an excellent launchpad and mission guidebook for your organization's data-driven journey."
Kirk Borne, Chief Science Officer, DataPrime

"Jordan Morrow writes brilliantly, engages with the reader and, most crucially, demystifies the world of data and analytics. It all makes sense, even for those not familiar with the subject or struggling to understand. This book is a terrific start and for those passionate about business and success, essential!"
Mike Roe, CEO, Tensense.ai

Be Data Driven

*How organizations
can harness the power of data*

Jordan Morrow

KoganPage

First published in Great Britain and the United States in 2022 by Kogan Page Limited

2nd Floor, 45 Gee Street	8 W 38th Street, Suite 902	4737/23 Ansari Road
London	New York, NY 10018	Daryaganj
EC1V 3RS	USA	New Delhi 110002
United Kingdom		India

www.koganpage.com

Kogan Page books are printed on paper from sustainable forests.

© Jordan Morrow, 2022

The right of Jordan Morrow to be identified as the author of this work has been asserted by him in accordance with the Copyright, Designs and Patents Act 1988.

ISBNs
Hardback	978 1 3986 0656 2
Paperback	978 1 3986 0612 8
Ebook	978 1 3986 0655 5

British Library Cataloguing-in-Publication Data
A CIP record for this book is available from the British Library.

Library of Congress Cataloging-in-Publication Control Number
2022026511

Typeset by Integra Software Services, Pondicherry
Print production managed by Jellyfish
Printed and bound by CPI Group (UK) Ltd, Croydon, CR0 4YY

To my beautiful wife and wonderful children:
how could I get so lucky?

CONTENTS

ACKNOWLEDGMENTS

A book like this doesn't come about without help. I want to thank Kogan Page for giving me the opportunity to write my second book with them. I want to thank the staff and hands at Kogan Page who helped review and provide edits, feedback, and just overall support through the process of getting this book to the finish line. I also want to pay tribute to all the amazing voices and minds that are leading the charge for data and analytical thought leadership, strategy, and other aspects of this amazing field. Finally, and certainly not least, I want to thank my wife and children for their support of me writing a second book and for my career—I couldn't do it without them.

PREFACE

In my first book, *Be Data Literate: The data literacy skills everyone needs to succeed*, we tackled the enormous, yet powerful, world of data literacy. In this book, we take on a term and concept that grew ever more popular during the Covid-19 pandemic: being "data driven." In the world of data and analytics, there is not a one-size-fits-all solution for organizations. In this book, I endeavor to help organizations learn key concepts and principles that will allow them to be more data driven. I hope through this book, you as an individual, leadership, and organizations can learn principles and pillars that will lead to data-driven success.

PART ONE

Foundational

In this first section, we will set the foundation for the term "data driven." We will look at the data-driven world, the impact of Covid-19, tools and technologies, and what it means to be data driven.

into 1GB thumb drives, these would stretch across 184 million football fields. In 2020, the WEF estimated there would be 44ZB collected for that year (Saha, 2020).

This data explosion goes even further: IDC predicts that by 2025 that number will balloon to 175 zettabytes (Rack Solutions, 2018). It is no secret that Covid-19 altered entire countries and economies, our way of life. We went from doing things our usual way, where we were comfortable, to an understanding that organizations needed to harness the power of data as quickly as possible to not only combat the effects of Covid-19 but truly succeed in the future world. Data empowered organizations to make sounder decisions during the pandemic by providing better pictures of the situation. If done right, organizations could stem the tide of change and shift easier. But why did all this data come to be? What sparked it into existence and how did we go from a relatively small amount of data to the Everest-esque mountains of data that are bombarding organizations and economies around the world?

The evolution of data and data analytics

In the same *Forbes* article mentioned above, there are two paragraphs that hit the nail on the head: they describe the current time as an "information explosion." From smartphones to connected appliances, most of what we use generates data. However, Saha argues that the real reason for an increase in data is the growing use of data analytics. There's an automatic feedback loop of data analysis and automated responses to analytic decisions, which generates new insights, creates data and leads to more data analysis. Therefore, companies are collecting more data than ever to transform their business with data-driven decisions and compete effectively.

To help us understand the paragraphs above, I want to take a look at some of the ideas and thoughts mentioned therein as if you were a person who had never heard of these topics. The reason to approach it from this angle is that although we may feel we understand these pieces, there are always going to be things we can learn about each topic and how it is affecting our careers, lives, and organizations on a daily basis. To do so, I will break down certain topics to help each individual reader gain a solid footing, geared towards that understanding of how these technologies, understandings, and more can be based in the overall data-driven world and leading within it. Throughout each topic, you will find tips and pillars that can empower an organization to understand the different aspects necessary for data-driven success in our world.

Smartphones and social media

With the announcement of the iPhone in January 2007 (Mingis and Montgomery, 2021), the world had little idea (or maybe some of it did) of just what would happen to organizations. Suddenly, the interconnectedness of individuals and organizations across many different internet-driven areas helped to create a tidal wave of new possibilities in data. Sure, the BlackBerry and Palm had connectedness, but not like this. Now, we had a business tool that could take users to the internet, allowing for myriad possibilities, one of which was the ability to shop online at any time when connected to the internet. Think of how often you as an individual go to Amazon or other user-friendly apps and sites on your phone to make a purchase. I know I personally do it all the time. In fact, I will make purchases more often on my phone than anywhere else. This new influx of data to a business is an interesting turning point in our data-driven world.

The influx of data to a business, when shown to the owners, analysts, marketing, and so forth, helped to build out trends, insights, and show patterns that were congruent to running a business more effectively. This is just one stream of data flooding into a business because of a smartphone.

The second potential insight regards the behavioral patterns of individuals on the smartphone itself, which can then be utilized for data-driven understanding of people and how they operate. This has become very valuable real estate for businesses, as it taps into an even deeper level of behavior than just purchasing behavior. Now, that said, this also led to the discovery of the inappropriate use of social media data, as seen in the documentary *The Great Hack* (2019), which has become a hot topic in our data-driven economy. Data ethics and governance will be addressed later in the book.

Sensors or the Internet of Things

Internet of Things (Oracle, 2021):

> ... the network of physical objects—"things"—that are embedded with sensors, software, and other technologies for the purpose of connecting and exchanging data with other devices and systems over the internet. These devices range from ordinary household objects to sophisticated industrial tools. With more than 7 billion connected IoT devices today, experts are expecting this number to grow to 10 billion by 2020 and 22 billion by 2025.

In the movies, it seems as if we are always seeing scenes where something causes a refrigerator, toaster, or something else to wake up and want to take over someone's life. Now, that is fictional and not necessarily what businesses are doing with the sensors they are planting within devices around the world, but those sensors are a big driver for the data-driven world we live in. Of course, we are not speaking about the sensors that Hollywood fantasizes will take over the world, but we are speaking of sensors that can help organizations and leaders take their businesses to the next level. This next level can include better targeting of customers, understanding of trends and usage of products, and more. A few examples of the real-world application of sensors and devices can help anyone understand the data-driven world in which we live.

The smart home

In my personal life, I see the direct power of the Internet of Things when it comes to my own home. This type of technology powers many homes, and in my home alone we have Amazon Alexa, a smart fridge, a garage door that can be connected to the internet, allowing me to check if I have forgotten to put it down (which, of course, I never do), a sprinkler and irrigation system run by my phone and the internet, and a vacuum cleaner my wife can map an entire floor on and use to target specific areas, run via her phone. Our internet is run off nodes strategically placed throughout the house. There is one piece of technology I really want to speak about in terms of its power to provide data and information to others: my heating and air conditioning system, which is run by a small, round device that sits on my wall and runs off an app in my iPhone.

This heating and air conditioning device, which I absolutely love, is such a power tool for the collection, analysis, and use of data. Imagine all the behavioral information this device collects from me on a daily basis. I can set the temperature high for a few days while I am on vacation. If I know my family is going to be back before me, I can adjust. If I am sitting in my living room and want to adjust it, I will. Now, couple that with temperature data from outside, the weather, the rain (my sprinkler system will automatically delay its regular cycle if there is rain in the forecast), the snow, etc. This little device can collect all of this behavior from me and internalize it at the company that owns the device.

When I sign up to use this device (or when anyone does) I must remember that I am signing agreements to allow the data collection, monitoring, etc. By doing so, the organization collecting the data can then understand and target things not only in my home but in any other homes in the area that have this same device. They can collect sample population data and information, allowing the business to target products or ideas for a community. In some cases, depending on the agreements, they can sell that data to other companies. Now imagine there is a trend in the data, and it is found that, on average, right around 15 November is when my community starts to turn up its heat for the long projected time of winter. Maybe the data is sold to a local store or online retailer, telling them to have a winter sale on coats, gloves, and warm clothing. Yes, the interconnectedness of our devices, homes, and communities allows not only the business that owns a device but those it is contracted with to target and make our lives better (hopefully) with smart deals and incentives. Here we can see the power and opportunity of the data-driven world that we live in.

Fitness trackers

It is no secret that the boom in fitness trackers has correlated with the boom in data. Around the holidays and other big sale events, it is hard to not see a sale or advertisement for these devices. I personally have two watches that collect data for me: my Garmin watch for trail running and fitness activities, and an iWatch. In speaking of these devices and the sensors therein, let's discuss the ramifications for the data world itself and how the data can be utilized by businesses for ideas, marketing, and more. If you aren't starting to see that we truly live in a connected, data-driven world, and aren't seeing a desire to capitalize on it, we will keep working on you.

Regarding my devices, I want to speak about a specific race I ran in July 2021, called the Speedgoat 50k. This race encompasses around 32–33 miles of mountain terrain in the state of Utah. It also gives you around 11,000–12,000 feet of vertical gain and descent, with much of the race more than 9,000 feet above sea level. Needless to say, this race is one of the hardest ultra-marathons in the world.

During this race, I utilized my Garmin watch to track my run, but it wasn't only during my run that I used it; during my training, I was using devices to track and train with. These devices are gathering mountains and mountains of data that Garmin, or whatever tracker you may use, can then utilize to understand the trends, background, and behavior of the users. This can be from sleep, to pace, to mileage, to location, to heartbeat, to steps per minute, to who knows how many other metrics. This data can be compiled, just like the information for my smart home, and then either used by Garmin itself or shared out to those who have the legal contracts to gather this data. This can be utilized to sell gear and clothing, target advertisements, and more.

The use of devices and sensors is not new, but they are strong, strong contributors to the data-driven world. An article captures one critical part of this story. In December 2018, Propane, a digital experience and platform agency in San Francisco, wrote:

> Digital commerce, which is the buying and selling of goods and services using mobile networks and the Internet, is growing every year. To take full advantage of IoT, businesses must understand that the digital marketplace is entering its third wave. The third wave of digital commerce combines the elements of technology and human connection. Companies must focus on having their customers' digital experience include the best of the traditional experience. (Propane, 2018)

In order for the connectivity of data to truly work for these companies, they and their leadership cannot act in a robotic manner. Organizations must understand that the collection of behavioral data must then translate into a connected and wonderful customer experience within the organization. With the smart home, you cannot have all these connected devices and then miss the mark and sell swimsuits during the time when the weather turns cold (unless the data shows that people like to buy those on sale); with my fitness trackers, you can't advertise one sport's equipment when I obviously would not enjoy it. The connection of the human element to the data element cannot be oversold or overstated. This connection will be explored later in the book.

Connected vehicles, grids, and data artifacts

As we think of the connectedness of our lives in our homes and on our wrists with our watches, and finally on our phones with all the apps and technology present there, we can look at the systems around the world and their connectedness on a larger scale. We can start with something we are all familiar with: our vehicles.

Now, you may be asking, how is a vehicle connected to the internet a big deal? A connected vehicle can truly provide not just the driver with powerful information, it can also provide cities, economies, devices, and more with information that can bring safety and more for millions of people. With a connected vehicle, a scenario or example can show all of us, and especially leaders, the power of using the connectivity of what is seemingly a simple thing and turning it into the power of data and analytics.

Imagine you are driving a connected vehicle. This vehicle can update the owner and driver with different scenarios, such as potential issues with the car. Now, imagine that vehicle is connected to the grid of a city, so the driving patterns of the vehicle are shared and utilized to improve traffic and safety. Also, imagine this vehicle sharing information on the overall use of the vehicle with its maker: how often the seat belts are worn, gas usage, speeds traveled, and many more data points. This can be shared to make more effective and efficient cars, used to target advertising, and more. This one connected vehicle can also communicate with the other vehicles around it. Imagine if a car can communicate a slowdown in traffic to other vehicles that are a few miles back, or warn of a dangerous situation. If weather conditions change and this is shared with other vehicles, it can prep drivers for inclement weather. The connectedness of a vehicle is just a simple step to potentially better driving and more effective safety.

Data-driven strategy and more

With all these amazing devices and the connected world, regardless of how amazing all of this data is, how wonderful and perfect it seems, we must remember one key thing: data is just data, and without a force moved against it, it is not going to produce the fruit and results we want as an individual or as an organization. To be a truly data-driven world, we need data strategies to bring results to our work, thoughts, and ideas. How do we do this? To start, let's turn back to what would have driven all this production of data in the first place: a strategy. Now, that said, just because a strategy was in place doesn't mean it was a strategy to drive data, but in the end a strategy is what is needed to drive a truly data-driven market and world. We will tackle building your own data-driven strategy later in the book, but for now

I want to speak to the overall need to have a data-driven strategy and the purpose thereof.

In my experience over the years, I have had the opportunity to travel the world, working with organizations of all shapes and sizes, speaking at conferences, and interacting with wonderful people. This has been a great opportunity for me, but it also opened up the door for me to really learn and understand the trends and opportunities therein. In that work, there are a few things that you learn and notice, which will be covered throughout the book:

1 There is a large gap in the understanding of the four levels of analytics: descriptive, diagnostic, predictive, and prescriptive. You can find more information on the four levels of analytics in my book *Be Data Literate: The data literacy skills everyone needs to succeed* (Morrow, 2021).

2 The skills gap in data is very present.

3 Organizations are spending money on powerful tools and technologies in the world today, but the return on investment for those tools is not as high as organizations would like (unfortunately, tools and technologies get blamed for the low adoption rate, when in reality it is the lack of data literacy skills).

4 There is a large gap in data strategies to enable an organization to harness its power with data.

Data-driven strategy: the need

In a conversation with a former colleague and executive, I asked a very direct question with regards to a data strategy: how many companies have a true data strategy? With all of the money being spent in data and analytics, with many revenue or total market projections out there—a quick Google search would show that it is over \$215.7 billion—one would think a sound and solid data and analytics strategy would be beneficial (Business Wire, 2021). In this conversation with my colleague, he mentioned that if he were to ask 10 executives what their data strategy is, all 10 would say they are moving their data to the Cloud. Three of them would know why they are moving it to the Cloud, the other seven wouldn't.

There are two issues with this: 1) moving data to the Cloud is not a true data and analytics strategy. It is an operation to improve storage and cost-effectiveness, but it is a piece of the puzzle, a tool to enable the true data and analytics strategy; and 2) the fact that seven of the executives wouldn't know why they are doing it is very disheartening. Now, you may ask yourself, is 10 a large enough sample? The answer is absolutely not. We weren't conducting this as a scientific study, it was a conversation between friends and colleagues. But, and there is a big but, through all my travels and experience of working with hundreds and hundreds of companies, which would be a large sample size, this total of 30 percent of companies understanding why they are importing data to the Cloud is going to be accurate and possibly too high.

In my travels, then, I have found an alarming trend that has continued now for years: organizations are not prepared, still, to truly succeed with data because they do not have a true data-driven strategy, a true data and analytical strategy. What I mean by this is that organizations have not put forth the effort, talent, hiring, investing, and an overall strategy that will allow them to accurately and successfully use their data to become data driven. In other words, organizations are not investing in and succeeding with data because their data-driven strategy leaves most of them not just found wanting but unfortunately falling very short. The overall lack of data-driven strategy is a big driver for low adoption rates with data and analytical work. It should also be a call for leadership to step up its efforts for success. It should be a big impetus for the "need" that exists for organizations and leadership all over the world.

Chief data officers (CDOs)

One reason there is a lack of data-driven strategy and success is the lack of investment in the right leadership: "In 2012, just 12% of Fortune 1000 companies had a CDO. By 2018, 67.9% of surveyed firms reported having a CDO" (Forbes Insights, 2019). One key part of this statistic is that these are the Fortune 1000; it is my experience that far fewer than almost 70 percent of all organizations have a CDO. In fact, the number becomes even lower when you evaluate organizations that don't have the CDO in the C-suite but reporting to another member of the C-suite, like a chief technology officer or chief information officer—another issue. I will unequivocally say you should not have a CDO reporting to another member of the C-suite. This shows that 1) you don't buy into the role fully enough to have them have a seat at the executive table; and 2) the C-suite member they report into will have their own agenda for technology, information, etc., and this can lead to conflicting priorities.

Overall, not having the CDO at the right spot at the table shows a weakness in a data-driven strategy. We must put them fully at the table to help them drive success across a true data-driven strategy and transformation. By having the CDO in the right position, the cultural shifts that need to occur can be led within the organization.

Along with the need for a CDO, a true data and analytical strategy is necessary to tie directly back to the business strategy. That's what it is—a support position. The tools that turn analytics and data into insight for decisions are just that, tools for enacting the business strategy. I will also add here unequivocally: data tools are not a strategy, they are an enabler of the strategy. We will explore more on the tools in a later chapter in this book.

A personal story or two can shed light on what I am seeing by way of leadership, learning, strategy, and more, and all of it hints at the need I am discussing. I want to discuss the trends and use specific examples.

Story 1: A learning strategy without the company's strategy

In 2021, I was invited to review an organization's learning strategy when it came to data. This was a financial firm specializing in insurance. As the organization wanted to become more data driven and empower its employees correctly with data, I was walked through the data learning strategy. Unfortunately, one key point kept returning and returning, and so I started to ask: what is your organization trying to do with data? How does this data learning strategy tie to your organization's overall data strategy? As I kept asking, the answer came back that they did not know. Their learning strategy and training could look great, with all the bells and whistles, but it came down to them not knowing what their business was doing with data and/or how this learning strategy tied to the business's strategy with data. This is a big problem. Without knowing that, how can the organization succeed and utilize data correctly? How can it be data driven if the data learning that is being put in place may not tie to what the organization is doing with data, given those leading the charge didn't know what the organization was doing with data?

Story 2: "We have data scientists but they are not being utilized"

Another story comes from 2019 when an organization brought me in to discuss data literacy and an overall strategy for its data use and learning. This was another financial institution, located and head-quartered in the United States and one of the most well known in the world. As I met with the group that brought me in, at the request of their chief learning officer, it was brought up to me that the organization had hired a data scientist for each business unit within the organization. The problem was they were not being utilized. The organization had done what many organizations may have done: data scientists are the "sexy" job and so they were hired in, but the company didn't know what to do with them. Thankfully this organization had hired a leader in data and was creating a center of excellence, and I was being brought in to help build a charge and change with data learning. Without that holistic strategy and leader, this organization would have been experiencing what many organizations experience: hiring and spending a lot of money, but not receiving a good return on investment.

Data-driven strategy: the skills and technology gap

Along with the need for a strategy, in order for an organization to succeed at being data driven and for the strategy to work, the organization must, and I repeat must, close its overall talent skills gaps. In studies on data literacy, a significant skills gap has emerged. One study that came out from Qlik showed that only around one out of five employees were confident in their data literacy skills. Twenty-five percent said they were fully prepared to use data effectively (Qlik, 2020). For organizations to truly succeed in being data driven, the skills gap needs to be closed. Someone may ask: what is the skills gap?

The skills gap contains two primary areas of concern for an organization: data literacy skills and technical data skills. The data literacy skills are the confidence to use data to find insight for decisions. The ability to work with data, to analyze it, to comprehend it and what you are looking at, and maybe most importantly, the ability to tell the overall story and picture of data. The skills gap doesn't necessarily only mean data literacy, it means employees need to be able to use the tools and data the company is investing in. Data tools, such as Tableau, Qlik, and Alteryx, are powerful, but without a combined skill set of data literacy and technology, we will continue to see the low adoption rates I have seen in my travels around the world.

Along with the gaps mentioned above, one key thing that needs to be understood is that there is a technology gap and debt within organizations wanting to succeed truly as data driven. What do I mean by this?

First and foremost, when an organization buys a tool or technology for use with data, what my experience shows is that the salespeople usually did a really good job of selling the ways in which a tool can perform, and it performed great. The problem with this? Of course the tool performed great; it was being used with a manicured data set, where the bugs are worked out, things go easily, and the magnificence of the tool is showcased. This selling of the tool and its perfect form is wonderful, but when the tool gets onsite and people try to implement it, it doesn't go the way the rep showed. What's more, you may see organizations buy 10,000 of these licenses. Well, with the skills gap being what it is, and the tool not working as well as it could, we see a weak adoption rate, hindering the power of a data-driven strategy.

The area I want to discuss deals with the term "technical debt."

ProductPlan (2021) discusses technical debt (also known as tech or code debt) as the result of development teams' actions in attempts to expedite a process or functionality delivery, which leads to later refactoring. In short, it's the effects of prioritizing fast delivery over quality of the code.

Now, this is technical debt and has been used to coin a new term: "data debt." I want to create another new term: "data-driven debt." Data-driven debt, like technical debt, is the debt that is accumulated over time from not having a proper data-driven strategy in place that is tied to your business strategy. This debt can accumulate because organizations continually invest in data tools and technology, hire data scientists for the sake of having them, do not have a CDO, use tools as the strategy, don't have a strategy tied to the business, etc. One can look into an organization very easily and see whether there is data-driven debt or not. In my experience, organizations are trying to dig themselves out of heaps of data-driven debt. One problem is that they keep thinking they are digging out of the debt only to find themselves piling the dirt over their shoulder and right back into the same hole.

Data-driven strategy: what's next?

With all this talk of a data-driven world, data-driven strategy, etc., one could ask: what's next? What is the direction of the data and analytical world? Will we become more data driven? Will the technology continue to evolve?

There are many books, articles, etc. that cover the different tools, technologies, and advancements that are taking place all over the world. Instead, we are going to talk about the future of being a data-driven organization. With that in mind, let's focus on the data-driven organization, specifically the people of the organization, and how this book will help the organization and its leadership to implement the necessary work and changes to succeed in this future world.

Data-driven workforce

Undoubtedly, the world is going to continue to march forward, driven by data and information. Tools and technologies are going to eat up this data, simplifying the processes and work that individuals need to do, and in the end, advancements will come and hit the economies and organizations of the world at a rapid pace. The key for an organization to succeed in this data-driven world is the workforce itself.

The organization must have a data-literate workforce, in its talent and culture, that can help leadership succeed with the data investments. To begin, leadership is the key to all of this. The data-driven world is going to march ahead and those organizations whose leadership is strong on data literacy, data strategy, data investments, and data technologies will thrive, as long as the culture keeps up and is ready to succeed. Leaders must invest in their own learning, as they must be data literate, and they must have the strategy, tools, people, and technology necessary for data-driven success. This includes the culture. Chapter 8 of this book helps to shape the culture of the organization, which we will think of as a four-legged stool made up of beliefs, energies, traditions, and accountability. With these four key characteristics, the ability to drive them with strength and data is necessary.

Beyond the leadership, the workforce must work through their skills gaps, must look to upskill and reskill themselves to be able to absorb the data-driven world and data-driven consumption the world is giving to them. Upskilling is the training up of an employee in the role they currently occupy, and reskilling is training someone in a new skill to transfer them to a new position. The holistic puzzle of the correct skills and needs of the organization, driven by the data-driven strategy, will dictate how a workforce flows. This will include the hiring of new talent. This overall strategy is fluid, data driven, and will help the organization's workforce to succeed over time.

Conclusion

With the world advancing and growing at great pace, where technology is advancing, growing, and changing on a regular basis, the use of data is going to grow and become even more ubiquitous in our lives. As organizations look to succeed in the economy of the future, the use of data, analytics, and the proper data-driven strategy is necessary. In this chapter I shared two examples of problems causing a lack of data-driven success. In reality, there are many, many reasons organizations are not succeeding with data. Changes and shifts need to occur for organizations to become powerful in a data-driven world. It is not too late for you or your organization to succeed here. Are you willing to do what it takes? To make the investment in time, talent, money, and energy to make it happen? Come join us in this journey to become a truly data-driven organization.

2

The impact of Covid-19 on organizations and data

The year 2020 is one that will live in the history books. These types of events—Covid-19—are ones that go down in history. As when I was a kid and would learn about the Great Depression in the United States that hurt the economy at the end of the 1920s going into the 1930s, generations will learn about the Coronavirus pandemic that wreaked havoc on the world. This pandemic took lives, shut down businesses and economies, and people had to learn how to survive with many people under one roof. People will read of the impacts— economically, physically, emotionally and through the lives and eyes of those who lived and experienced it. Every single day, we were hit on the news with charts, data, terminology, and more. One thing that certainly can and should be discussed is the information, misinformation, and misuse of data throughout the pandemic. These egregious acts were rampant, irrespective of political party or ideology. I have said many times that the pandemic was one of the greatest illustrative examples of the need for data literacy. The world, businesses, and we as individuals were inundated daily with huge amounts of data and information. How were we to handle all of this?

The reality is, a lot of people may have been flooded by more data and information than they ever thought necessary. Organizations were also flooded by new amounts of data and information; remote work, economic shutdowns, government policy and more impacted organizations in many ways. What did this information overflow do to organizations? What kind of impact did the pandemic have on the future of organizations? The purpose of this chapter is to help the reader understand the impact the pandemic had on organizations, what leadership can learn from these situations, and finally, areas and tips that organizations and leaders can use to overcome obstacles. To do this, I will utilize personal examples of my work with organizations before and throughout the pandemic. By using real-world examples from my life, I hope to bring context and understanding to the reader, showing the scenarios and impacts.

World experience

I spoke a bit about this in the last chapter, but I want to expand on my personal schedule and work life. Organizations have been investing in data for years, this is no secret. What does it mean to invest in data? Organizations can invest in data in many ways. Pre-pandemic, organizations were buying business intelligence tools, sourcing data into data warehouses, using the Cloud, and using different tools and technologies in various ways. Unfortunately, through my experience working with organizations of different shapes and sizes, in different industries and regions, I have seen that organizational investments in data and technology fall far short of success. By short, I mean these organizations were not experiencing or receiving the return on investment they would have hoped for.

To understand why this matters, it should be noted that poor data quality costs the US economy up to $3.1 trillion yearly (Petrov, 2021). If I were a leader in an organization that was either 1) spending a lot of money on data tools and technology, or 2) losing large amounts of money, I would want to know and remedy the situation as soon as possible.

Personal schedule

With the thoughts around organizations and investments in data and analytics on our mind, let's take a look at my work schedule a bit more and why it blew up in a tornado of busyness. At the time, my work calendar was spent meeting with and hearing from organizations such as those described above. In spending all this time with organizations, I noticed that certain trends or patterns emerged. Some of the key learnings were:

1 The number one roadblock to data and analytics success is the culture of the organization.
2 The data literacy skills gap is a barrier to being data driven.
3 The data literacy skills gap is a key to overcoming the gaps and becoming data driven.
4 Investments in tools and data are ubiquitous throughout the world.
5 No region or industry is doing better than another.
6 Organizations do not have strong data strategies (although many thought they did).

While these are big trends, these are just some of the key trends and patterns that emerged throughout the pandemic.

My work calendar can be seen as divided between two time periods: pre-pandemic and after the pandemic started. As I worked with these organizations pre-pandemic, I spent my time helping them to build data literacy strategies, holding thought leadership webinars, speaking at conferences, and helping organizations with their data and analytical needs. This was time well spent, as organizations truly were enthusiastic about data, but like a lot of things, we cannot see our blind spots or gaps in where we should be working and emphasizing our work. As I continued to work with these organizations, and as the year 2020 moved on, I expected my time to open up as travel was restricted, economies and businesses shut down, and overall, my schedule from a "normal" perspective worked and evolved. Unfortunately this was not what happened.

As the pandemic began and started to close organizations' doors to in-person work and normal operations, as economies looked to ensure the health and well-being of the individuals living therein, and as organizations looked to pull the different data-driven levers they would need to succeed, certain things started to happen; I will speak about this in a minute. During this unprecedented time, my focus also looked to change. I went into a mode of helping organizations and doing whatever I could to further data literacy to help individuals and organizations around the world. While my travel lessened, the unexpected occurred: my schedule got busier and busier. One would think that without a schedule traveling the world, my time would open up. This presented interesting use cases for us to understand and has opened up a door for this book to illustrate how to be data driven.

There is one key thing that needs to be noted about my career. While I may have worked for a data technology vendor, I was product agnostic, so I had non-customers and customers alike wanting help and to have discussions on data literacy. This was pivotal to my schedule opening up more and more.

To begin our understanding of the pandemic's impact on businesses, I feel it will be more beneficial if we look at different companies and use cases. By reading stories of things that happened during the pandemic, you may be able to see things happening in your own roles and companies that you can relate to. I will be using specific companies, although not by name, to look at individual trends. I may also aggregate businesses or industries together. We will also look at the impact of the news on the pandemic, and how it could have affected the organizations and businesses in a particular region. Finally, we can look at the "what could have been" approaches to being data driven. Again, with this book, I want us to look at all of this through the lens of being data driven.

We will also look at different regions and economies in the world. While the nature of shutdowns varied across the world, the need for and use of data is paramount and universal. This is an interesting subject to consider because of how different economies and countries handled the pandemic.

The retail industry

One industry impacted greatly by the Covid-19 pandemic was the retail industry. The first organization I will speak about also has a large presence in the entertainment industry. This is especially important to note, as this organization has many branches in the retail industry (think entertainment company that sells merchandise). The pandemic shut doors, changed practices, and forced these businesses to shift their way of doing business. This was a hard shift that wasn't driven slowly but came overnight.

This organization in particular came to me with the thought of improving its data literacy. It pulls in billions and billions of data points on a consistent basis, and is one of the largest organizations in the world. It has its arms and branches in many different industries and fields, thereby necessitating a large and complex use of data. Imagine an organization whose main goal is entertainment, but drives retail and other areas. These different business units have different targets and goals, and with that, the use of data is critical throughout the organization.

This organization reached out to me, not as a customer of the company I worked for, with a need for data literacy. As seen by many organizations at this time, the organization couldn't do all it wanted to do to succeed with data; it wasn't in a position to be data driven. This theme was consistent with the various retail organizations I was chatting with at the time. Organizations wanted to pull the right levers, but it was not possible. The pandemic illuminated the internal skills gap and the need to use data more.

A second organization was mainly focused on retail apparel itself. What is interesting is that this organization reached out to me on two different fronts, from two different points within the organization, with regards to its data. One of the issues that existed before the pandemic, and was probably illuminated even more because of the pandemic, was not having a centralized strategy around data. Multiple people from multiple spots in the organization reaching out for the same thing, but not knowing that the others are, is a gap. This is an interesting thing in this regard: the strategy and use of data. This organization has over 70,000 employees, with probably many different data teams, data sets, and so forth. Because of the size of the company, the many different uses of data, a data strategy could be difficult to disseminate through the organization. As the pandemic inched forward, it helped to drive these strategy wedges wider and to light up these data holes that existed within the organization.

What is really interesting about this organization is that one of the individuals that reached out to me was from a centralized data team for the entire organization. The other individual was trying to pioneer and drive a data literacy strategy within the organization. The lines of communication were not in place to help drive and ensure solid governance over strategy and work. That said, this organization was actually in a good position, ahead of many others during the pandemic or just before. While many organizations were dipping their toes in the water, this organization was putting forth an effort to become data driven.

Supply chain

When speaking with regards to the supply chains around the world, it can safely be said that the global Covid-19 pandemic not only disrupted supply chains but altered them for the future. One key thing to understand with regards to supply chains around the world is the global world and economy we live in. Whether we want to think that way or not, we live in a truly globalized world. Therefore, when economies shut down, when supplies became scarce, when organizations couldn't receive their products, then we saw the true impact and why the use of data becomes more than a nice to have. We see the true nature of needing to be data driven.

For supply chain organizations to be truly data driven, it requires the right framework, culture, and more. What we see coming from the pandemic with regards to supply chain is a robust data strategy so the use of data is ubiquitous throughout a supply chain organization, and not going off gut feel or human instinct alone.

In an Ernst & Young article from February 2021, we can see some of the changes to be made to supply chain organizations. Some of these are (Harapko, 2021):

1 Increase efficiency
2 Retrain/reskill workforce
3 Manage/reduce costs

Each one of these areas of emphasis, and there are more, is riddled with data, thereby necessitating the work for supply chain organizations to be more data driven. To do so, these organizations will have a substantial increase in reskilling and retraining the workforce.

Along with the issues mentioned above, the overall securing and improving of supply chains will be crucial in the future. To do this, supply chain organizations will be utilizing the power of data and the insight found therein, especially during the global pandemic, to make decisions on how to secure the chain for breakage. Unfortunately, during the pandemic, these organizations experienced massive disruptions the likes of which they may never have seen before. As such, these organizations have to now make data-driven decisions to succeed and ensure continuity into the future.

The media and news

This is a very sensitive subject when it comes to the Covid-19 pandemic, especially when it deals with political affiliation. I want to make clear that when I talk about Covid-19 and its impact in the media and news, in the lives of businesses, I will refrain from stating what is right or wrong, what should and shouldn't be done. I will also not mention political parties in specificity. We want to examine the use of data through these organizations during the pandemic and how it impacted or could have impacted lives and organizations across the globe.

It is no secret that businesses and individuals were looking to the data being presented to them to help them drive a data-driven business during uncertain times, and they should have. Organizations should pull internal AND external data to truly be data driven. The issue is not the desire to pull in data to make smarter, well-informed decisions. It is the misuse of data within the media that can cause a real stir.

A *Medium* article from the beginning of the pandemic, and this was in the very early stages, illustrated for readers the misuse of data (Leybzon, 2020). We can then share why this misuse would impact organizations looking to be data driven. In the article, it says there were three misuses of data during the pandemic:

1 Distorted y-axis—cutting down the y-axis to make something appear worse than it is.
2 Correlations and causations—a big no no: correlation does not equal causation.
3 A failure to normalize—where we do not normalize data to make it apples to apples.

As you can imagine, as the pandemic progressed on and on, organizations would hear these news stories, this information, and have to make smart, data-driven decisions. It became very difficult for organizations looking to use data to shore up and secure their business during this very uncertain and difficult economic time, to decipher what was real and what wasn't. As models were presented, some shared time and time again, some were recanted or restated. We saw predictions shift and change over and over. This can create a confusing cacophony, making it very hard to find the signal amongst the noise.

One thing to note: these issues are not only prevalent in the media and news fields; we are inundated with the misuse or poor use of data on a regular basis. I remember flying during a business trip and seeing a gentleman across the aisle reading a newspaper. This was a supposedly very reputable newspaper, one of the best known in the financial world. This publication had distorted the y-axis to make the graphic look worse than it was. These issues—the failure to use the full y-axis, assuming correlation means causation, and the failure to normalize—are all symptoms of larger problems; companies are not truly data driven or data literate. Because of this, the pandemic could make it difficult for a company to make a smart, data-driven decision because the use and reliability of data may be non-existent.

Financial industries

I want to share a personal experience to draw upon the use of data within an organization during trying and recession-like circumstances. In a prior career life, I worked in a financial organization during the financial crisis and recession of the late 2000s. During this time, the organization absolutely utilized data closely to try to make smart decisions on what to do. In my role, I was analyzing delinquency and write-off rates. To do so, I had to pull data sets into my modeling. That modeling was then utilized to help analyze these important numbers and rates during a trying time. During Covid-19, the use of data should have been paramount to organizations' success.

During the pandemic, the same thing would be seen across organizations. One big issue would be present: the ability for an organization to succeed with data and pull the right levers to ensure the longevity of the organization. For me, I was pulled into helping a financial services organization drive the right reskilling and culture. This organization had started to shape itself pre-pandemic, only to find itself not ready and in survival mode. This is a standard scenario for financial organizations; survival mode during a crisis is the modus operandi. This is not fully data driven as it should be. This is more about using the data to drive a descriptive analytic, describing what is happening, to then direct a decision. Unfortunately, the other three levels of analytics are not at the forefront as much as they should be.

Another financial organization I worked with is from the insurance space. This company was trying to be more data driven and was building and implementing a large learning program for upskilling or reskilling the workforce, especially to use data. As I went through the organization's learning program, one common theme kept coming up over and over: I would ask, "What is your organization's data strategy?" They couldn't answer this question. I told them they needed to go back to the drawing board to ensure their learning strategy matched the data strategy. First and foremost, the individuals building the learning plan needed to know the data strategy. This is another prevalent issue in organizations: the individuals and employees of the company not knowing the overall data strategy. Without that knowledge, an organization's ability to succeed can be severely hampered.

Industry and organization summary

With businesses within these industries and others looking to advance in the world of data and analytics, Covid-19 set forth patterns and trends that changed the data and analytics industry forever. We can see some of these trends within the examples above, but we want to drive a concise list for you, the reader, to have on your mind as you study this book and what it takes to be a data-driven organization. The list is as follows:

- Adapting and building the right data-driven culture is crucial to the success of an organization.
- Organizations are investing in upskilling and reskilling initiatives to ensure they can compete in the future economy.
- Investment in data tools and technology is rising, including an increase in movement of data to the Cloud.
- Every region and industry around the world is being pushed to be data driven.
- Data and analytical strategies and the hiring of leaders to lead these data strategies are on the rise.

These trends each represent shifts or sped-up trends that were already in motion, albeit not at a rate that was necessary for data-driven work, and through these trends we can get a glimpse of what organizations and leadership can do to succeed with data. Let's share a brief and sound summary of each of these trends and why they are in such demand and necessary for organizations to be data driven.

Culture

How did the data culture of organizations shift during the Covid-19 pandemic? Let's first examine a little on data culture. *Tableau* describes data culture as the collective behaviors and beliefs of people who encourage using data for improved decision making. Consequently, data runs throughout the operations, mindsets and identity of an organization and its people and this culture enables everyone to tackle complex business challenges with data-driven insights.

Through an organization's culture, you will find the most important aspects and drive for an organization to be successful as a data-driven culture. As data has been democratized, making digital information accessible to the average non-technical user of information systems without requiring the involvement of IT, if the organization culture isn't in place to help bring those traditions, ideas and more to work, it creates a roadblock for an organization to become data driven. We think of technology, the data, the hard skills, as the big keys to success. The reality is, the culture of the organization will either enable or impede the success of being data driven.

Upskilling and reskilling the workforce

One of the great needs that became more transparent during the pandemic was that of upskilling and reskilling the individuals and workforces in organizations. This is one of the impetuses for data literacy, the field I helped pioneer with Valerie Logan and others. To help us understand these two areas, let's explore how these terms are described to try and achieve better clarity on what they mean.

According to Merriam-Webster, "upskilling" is providing further education or training to develop employees' skills (Merriam-Webster, 2021). On the other hand, Cambridge Dictionary describes "reskilling" as acquiring new or different skills to those currently used in order to undertake a different job or task (Cambridge Dictionary, 2021).

Hopefully, through these two definitions, it is becoming clearer. To upskill someone is to train them, within their current role, on new skills that will enable them to do their job better or more easily. To reskill, or reskilling, is to train someone to do a totally different job, as opposed to training them up with new skills within a current role. To illustrate, let's look at two different employees and then dig into what Covid-19 did to drive upskilling and reskilling within the fields of data and analytics.

Let's picture a marketing employee named Lauren. This marketing analyst needs to work within her domain more closely with data. Her organization has invested in sound Cloud strategies and storage for data. They have purchased thousands of business intelligence tools to help her visualize and find insight in the data. There is only one problem: Lauren didn't go to school to learn how to operate and utilize these tools and technologies. This problem is shared by many of her employees; the data and technology are being invested in to help them succeed with a new data-driven strategy, but the majority of them didn't go to school to use data at this company. There is some familiarity, but it falls short of the desired effect. Lauren's organization has set out to build a data literacy learning program to upskill its workforce, empowering them to succeed with data.

The second employee we will look at is named Mark. Mark went to school and studied to work in the retail industry. As Mark progresses in the retail industry, he is noticing that many of the jobs he has done can now be done by algorithms, data, and technology. So, Mark goes out to study roles in data and analytics, which is a field growing at an incredible rate. Mark sees so much potential to succeed in this space, but in this case, he needs to study a different field than his own, thereby reskilling himself to be able to succeed in this space.

The Covid-19 pandemic led to the need to upskill and reskill many employees if an organization desired to be truly data driven. Organizations saw the need to change because of the pandemic. This became a necessity as organizations failed to be data driven during the pandemic, or fell short of their desired state. Because of this, organizations have been deploying data literacy and learning strategies to coincide with their data and/or business strategies.

One big tip and word of caution to leaders who have to lead their organizations to be data driven: to ensure your work succeeds, get to the root of your data literacy and analytical needs with regards to skill in your organizations. Whether you look to attack through hiring of new skills, the upskilling and reskilling of employees, or a combination of both, part of your data-driven strategy has to be a learning strategy to empower and enable your workforce to succeed with data.

Invest in the right data tools and technology

This isn't necessarily a new trend, as organizations, individuals, and economies all over the world have been investing in data tools and technology for years. An article in *Forbes* in 2020 showed that in artificial intelligence alone, more than $50 billion was going to be spent (Jeans, 2020). That is an incredible amount of money, and that is just in artificial intelligence. This does not even show us what was going to be spent on business intelligence tools, the Cloud, and so forth.

The right investments in the right data and analytical tools and technology are necessary for organizations to be truly data driven. For leadership, this can be a pivotal point in a journey. As the organization looks to source its data, to drive its lineage (which I define as the sourcing of data through to its use for insight), and to utilize its data, the right tool needs to be in place, but it has to be done right.

One of the trends you could find throughout organizations around the world—and these gaps looked to be shown through the Covid-19 pandemic—was an investment in tools that were not adopted at the rate leadership would like. An example from my career can illuminate what I am discussing.

In a prior role, I had the opportunity to use an internally built business intelligence tool. While we used this tool, we created strong and successful work. Then, whether it was a wonderful salesperson who sold the company on the power of a business intelligence tool (which I won't name) or a vice president looking to set their bonus and foundation on this investment, we were told we needed to migrate to the newly invested-in business intelligence tool. I consistently said that as long as we could reproduce what we had done within the new tool, I was ok with it. After a year of trying, they could not do it. This issue can be seen around the world within organizations: invested-in business intelligence and data tools are not effectively implemented and/or adopted.

Salespeople do a great job of selling their power, with perfectly manicured data sets. Of course the tool will work when the perfect data set that is used to demo the tool is utilized, but when it is utilized against the organization's data, it does not work. This lack of "working" and the gaps that it causes are a big problem within data and analytics. During the pandemic, you could see organizations trying to utilize data and the tools they need, only to fall short. This trend of investing in the right tools and technology is necessary, partnered with data literacy learning, to ensure data-driven success.

Every region and industry is being pushed to be data driven

This comes as no secret, but during the pandemic, it became more and more apparent that every region, industry, economy—basically everything—needed to become data driven. I think this became very obvious as the pandemic progressed and regions and countries around the world shut down, necessitating the use of data and analytics to make decisions on what they should do to succeed during the pandemic.

Not only was this an issue for economies that shut down, but the organizations and leadership within these regions, from small to large, needed to use data for success. Most, if not all, readers of this book will know a restaurant, local business, etc. that was affected by the pandemic. These businesses needed to start to use data and information on the pandemic to know how to run effectively. This was across the world. Businesses needed to take on more and more information to make smarter, more effective decisions. This need to be data driven was new for some, if not a lot of organizations. They had been local, surviving on the power of business and the citizens working in the area, but now, it was necessary to use the information pouring out from the pandemic. This data-driven approach became a "here to stay" approach.

Data strategies and hiring of leaders

The TRUE use of a data strategy is now in effect. The reason I emphasize the word "true" is because a lot of organizations thought they were using data strategies, but they weren't. A data strategy is a strategy in the use of data that supports the overall business strategy. This aspect is too soon forgotten. Historically, these two things—a business and a data strategy—were seen as or used apart from each other. That cannot be anymore. These two strategies work hand in hand. The data strategy should be there to support the overall strategy of an organization.

Along with the true use of a data strategy, the hiring of leaders to lead on data and analytics is now officially in place for organizations. Because of the Covid-19 pandemic, it should no more be seen that you can just have a vice president or someone in the organization to lead on a data strategy. It should be seen that an organization needs an executive specifically for this. This individual should be a member of the C-suite, such as a chief data officer or chief analytics officer. These roles need to be seen as vital within an organization. To tip toe through it is not going to help an organization be successful with data.

Conclusion

I am sure a lot, if not the vast majority of us, are exhausted by the amount of data being shown to us on a regular basis. Daily updates, new numbers, the sad toll of the deaths that were presented to us, could become tiresome. The Covid-19 pandemic drove more data usage and conversations than maybe any other topic. With that in mind, it also became the most illustrious example of the need for data literacy in the world, maybe ever. It was also an amazing example of the need to have a data-driven organization. Many changes came to the world of business, to the economies of the world, and to our individual lives. To help combat the pandemic and the issues that were presented, the need to be data driven is now here to stay.

3

Technologies advancing data and analytics, and the need for the human element

It is no secret that organizations all over the world are spending money on technologies to help them with data and analytical work. It isn't just spending money—they are spending A LOT of money. In a 2019 CNBC article, it was said that tech spending would near $4 trillion that year (Rosenbaum, 2019). That is trillion with a "t." A *Forbes* article from 2020 said that companies would spend $50 billion on artificial intelligence that year (Jeans, 2020). Now, the title of the article has a bit more to it: "Companies will spend $50 billion on artificial intelligence this year with little to show for it." The last part of the title, "with little to show for it," says a lot. We will spend the latter part of this chapter capturing thoughts around these technologies and how the human element is essential for leadership to capture and utilize for their organizations to truly be data driven.

Tools and technologies

As the world of data and analytics has been shaped and molded over the years, these data and analytical tools and technologies that companies are spending so much money on have helped shape not only the success that organizations are seeing in data and analytics today but also the shortcomings, gaps, and pitfalls that are being experienced. Just like when a house is being built, there are different things that go into place, each one of them vital to the success of that house being built in the correct manner: the plans, architecture schematics, hammers, nails, wood, saws, cement, manpower, knowledge and skills, etc. If you look at the majority of the items being used to build that house, they are tools. Within the world of data and analytics it is the same. We need the tools and technologies to make it happen. That being said, the key element in all of it is not the tool or material but the human power and skill to make those things come to life. It is the same within the world of data and analytics. The human element is the key, the strength, the power that drives the creativity and decisions.

But for now, let's talk about the different technologies that are being invested in, shaped, created, invented, and utilized by organizations the world over. I feel like I hear about a new technology, well, this is a bit exaggerated, but on a daily basis. Do I truly hear about them that often? The answer is no, but I know new technologies are popping up and if they are popping up to me, leadership across organizations around the world is hearing more and more about different technologies often, especially from salespeople.

To help us understand and build out our knowledge of the technologies that are available today, I want to dive into different subsections of the tools and technologies that are available for individuals, leadership, and organizations. There are many data tools, all with different strengths and weaknesses. I want to make it clear that this will not be a chapter on which tools YOU should buy, but rather an objective view and look at technologies that are present in the world today. Also, this will not be a fully comprehensive list. The reality is, a whole book could be written on all the tools and technologies. In this book, I will present them in a view that defines what the tools are, shares examples of the different tools and technologies, what each type of tool different data personas will use, and I may even throw in examples of where this technology is being used. The different sections that I will cover are going to be shaped by what I will call data personas.

To ensure you have a good understanding of these tools, it is important you also understand what a data persona is. Data personas are the different roles within the world of data and analytics. Example data personas are:

- data scientist
- data analyst
- data engineer
- business user
- leadership

These are just a few examples of the different types of data personas that exist within the world of data and analytics.

The data tools, capabilities, and technologies we will cover are:

- business intelligence and data visualization
- data science
- coding languages
- artificial intelligence
- machine learning
- the Cloud
- databases
- data lakes
- human capital

These tools and technologies represent a wonderful opportunity for organizations and individuals to become successful and truly data driven. With the right investment in time, talent, and technology, an organization can harness the power to be data driven and succeed well into the future economy, with all its shifts and changes. Let's jump into these terms, tools and technologies to help drive a better understanding for you.

Business intelligence and data visualization

It is very appropriate that the first section we discuss in the world of tools and technologies within data and analytics is business intelligence and data visualization. I put these together because these tools of business intelligence and data visualization truly go hand in hand. It is these tools that the mass of users within an organization who have to use data and analytics see the most, every single day (think Microsoft Excel); every employee of every organization around the world is truly a data employee today and into the future. What is business intelligence exactly? How do we define data visualization? Let's solve these questions first and then we will talk about examples of these tools and technologies.

Business intelligence

Fruhlinger and Pratt (2020) discuss business intelligence, also known as BI, as intelligence-leveraging software and services to turn data into actionable insights. These insights can then contribute to an organization's strategy and business decisions. It can also refer to a range of specific BI tools that can access data set and present findings in reports, dashboards and chards to help users visualize the analysis.

I really like this definition of business intelligence that comes to us from CIO.com. In essence, business intelligence is the set of tools and technologies that are designed, built, and deployed throughout organizations to help democratize data to the masses. The democratization of data means to give and spread the use of data throughout the workforce. Democratizing data is a powerful way to get more eyes, ears, and voices into the data. Historically, organizations and leaders could deploy data and analytical work in a small set of employees or teams. With the advent of business intelligence tools and technologies, businesses can now invest and spread the use of data throughout an organization. Doing this empowers more eyes to be on the data, more backgrounds, experiences, etc. We will speak more to this as we discuss the human impact of these technologies and how they all work together, or at least should, in a symbiotic fashion to empower an organization to be data driven.

Data visualization

Now that we have defined what business intelligence is, let's put down the definition of data visualization, and you will see how they go hand in hand. Data visualization is "the graphical representation of information and data. By using visual elements like charts, graphs, and maps, data visualization tools provide an accessible way to see and understand trends, outliers, and patterns in data" (Tableau, 2021).

Data visualization is an area of data and analytics that has taken the world by storm. This may seem like an overreaction, but the reality is you can search out communities of data visualization specialists and even have them come at you when you work or talk about a different vendor than their preferred. The reality is, the world of data visualization has grown and become quite large and exciting, but there is a caution therein that leaders and organizations truly need to take heed of.

Over the past few years, the popularity of data visualization tools and the ability of salespeople to make them sing have made them extremely popular. It needs to be known that a data visualization tool is just that, a tool. Data visualization is not the be-all and end-all of analytics. It is just a piece of the puzzle. A tool that can be utilized to help organizations succeed with data. That's what a tool does: it helps organizations or individuals to succeed with a desired outcome. In this case, in data and analytics, a tool is there to help an organization drive data-driven analytical success. That is how data visualization and the tool that made it need to be viewed.

One may ask oneself, why are these tools so prevalent? It is true that these tools have become very popular and very successful, so why are we seeing so many of them pop up? Why are they so popular? The world of data and analytics can be intimidating and difficult to navigate. When the world is sitting on billions and billions of data points, it is necessary to have something to help simplify the use of data. Herein step the data visualization tools. These tools help to democratize data and bring it to the masses, which is essential as organizations want to become data driven.

Data science

"Data science" is a fascinating term and capability, and its use throughout organizations is essential in order for an organization to be truly data driven. What is data science and how does it operate? What is its place within a data and analytical strategy? Those are the questions we want to answer and discuss in this section. One item to note is that I will be writing about data science in its pure form. Unfortunately, the term data science has become muddied over time. Here, we will discuss it in the form of science.

DataRobot (2021) describes data science as a field of study encompassing programming skills, knowledge of mathematics and specific domain expertise, with the goal to extract useful insights from data. In essence, data science is the technical aspect of data and analytics, and it requires extra education, whether through experience or in a formal setting, to be able to use data science to drive insights and value from and in the data.

It can also help to distinguish what isn't data science. One big misnomer in the world of data and analytics is when individuals and organizations classify data visualization as the use of data science. While it is true that data visualization can be used to tell a story about the results from an analysis or hypothesis test, the visualization is not data science, it is the ability to visualize and use the analysis set in place. Within the world of data and analytics, data science involves more technical knowledge and background that moves beyond data visualization. Data visualization is powerful, but it is a step in the holistic process of data and analytics, and is not data science itself.

As leaders and organizations work towards becoming truly data driven, the use of data science in its proper form is a critical piece of the puzzle.

Coding languages

Uh oh, here come the technical coding languages. Within the world of data and analytics, does everyone in an organization need to learn how to code? As leadership puts into place strategies, use cases, and invests dollars into data and analytics, should everyone be able to code and read code? The answer is absolutely no, not everyone needs to learn how to code. This is crucial to understand so that strong, sound, and successful data strategies are put into place. Only a few will need to know how to code.

Three main coding languages utilized within data and analytics, particularly in the data science, ML and AI spaces, are R, Python, and SQL. Each of these coding languages is vital. Other popular languages include JavaScript, Java, C/C++, MATLAB, and Scala. Although this is not a comprehensive list, it shows some of the most popular and/or used programming languages that can empower an organization to be data driven.

What are coding languages used for within an organization and how can leadership and organizations utilize them for success? Coding, or programming, languages can be used for many facets of data. When it comes to use, manipulation (not necessarily a bad term within the world of data and analytics), cleansing, retrieval, statistical analysis and more, these languages can be utilized for organizations to be able to successfully use the tools presented to them.

One key thing for leaders and organizations to understand is that these languages are specific, technical, and utilized by a smaller subset of users within the organization. When leaders look to set forth strong and powerful data-driven strategies, it should be noted that they do not need to get every employee in the organization to learn these coding languages. Instead, the focus should be on those who have been tasked with using the languages and ensuring their training, background, and technology skills are up to date with the latest and greatest technologies present within programming and the tools where the languages are needed.

Artificial intelligence

We all need to run and hide because the world of robots is going to take over. Is that what you think of when you think of artificial intelligence?

IBM (Cloud Education, 2020) referred to John McCarthy's 2004 paper when they offered an insight into artificial intelligence as making intelligence machines and computer programs. While it can be similar to using a computer to understand human intelligence, the scope is not confined to biological observations.

Ok, so what in the world does that mean?

When we think of artificial intelligence, in essence it is driving machines to work and think like humans. That is the bare bones of AI. In the world of data and analytics, this can be especially powerful because of the power of computers to drive decisions, make calculations, solve problems, in shorter amounts of time than a human is capable of. This offers a lot of power for organizations to drive better insight work through data and analytics.

Artificial intelligence is deployed within data and analytics in different ways and understandings. Artificial intelligence is an empowerment of machines that enables them to learn within themselves, which can drive more processing and power within data. Now, I know I am simplifying this definition greatly, but it should provide the reader with a high-level understanding of a simplistic approach to AI. With that processing power, AI has the ability to process large amounts of data, automate tasks, and more. Through the referenced article from IBM, it can be learned that this is an ability to have the machine do what in the past were human-centered tasks. These tasks can include building data visualizations, predictive ordering of goods or services, or inputting food orders at restaurants. What an empowering tool and technology for data.

Once again, though, we cannot forget the power of the human element to drive the decision making behind this. What do I mean by this? While AI may be powerful in driving processes in data, helping to simplify things for the human from a process, calculation, and computation perspective, the decisions laid forward still need to be implemented or have a human element to them. Just like you can have machines building a house, they would need to be supervised to ensure in the end that things were built correctly. In data, as artificial intelligence builds out plans, processes analyses, and more, a human can be there to employ and deploy the different results and answers the artificial intelligence puts in place. This can help ensure biases, the decision itself, and more are correct and sound.

With the advent of artificial intelligence and the capability of machines to do the work for us, I think a story from my work with organizations around the world is helpful here.

I was traveling to South Africa to speak at a conference that I was invited to. The company putting on the conference had me visiting different customers or companies during my visit. Along with visiting other companies, the organization itself had me speak to some of its employees. In a meeting with them, a gentleman raised his hand and asked essentially this question: "Is all this intelligence just going to make us lazy?" That is an interesting question. With the machines able to do a lot of work for us, are we going to get lazy?

I flipped the question around a little on him. I brought up an example. Let's say that for each of us in our roles, it takes three hours to do a report or dashboard in our work. This could be a menial or uneventful amount of time, just boring and dull. Now, let's say an AI machine can build that dashboard or report for you in 15 minutes, what do you do with that extra two hours and 45 minutes that was just given to you? Do you sit still and be lazy? I flip it and say you now have two hours and 45 minutes to analyze, dig deep, understand, and find the necessary insight to make a decision. This is a power of the tool and technology: the freeing of time to do more meaningful work. We shouldn't be lazy, we should be empowered. There is a catch: the end users of the information, insight, etc., that the AI and machine present to us, need to be data literate in order for them to make a decision with the data. This is very important for overall holistic success through an organization with data, analytics, and AI: the overall data literacy and confidence the organization has in using data. We may have a wonderful machine to build analyses for us, but if the end users are not confident in their ability to use data, then it may fall short of the intended use and power.

A different power example of this comes from my time with Qlik, the business intelligence, data visualization, data integration, etc. vendor. During my time at Qlik, I had the opportunity to work with the R&D team to drive the tools' abilities to power intelligent building with the machine. One thing I loved in this area was helping the team develop the tool so it could recommend the types of charts that might be helpful and beneficial for the data set the end user was using. For example, let's say you have an end user who doesn't have much background or knowledge within data and analytics, having no idea where to start or which chart to use. Within the tool, the power was built to drive the suggested charts you should use. What a powerful way to start an individual's ability to use the tool to find insight in the data.

Overall, artificial intelligence, when used properly, can be a very powerful tool and technology for an organization looking to be data driven.

Machine learning

An article by IBM in 2020 provides a concise description of machine learning as a form of artificial intelligence and computer science that specifically concerns the use of data and algorithms to imitate how humans learn (IBM Cloud Education, 2020b). In essence, machine learning is where the machines themselves learn through the data and algorithms, improving on themselves as time goes on. I like to think of machine learning like working out and fitness. Over time, you learn and grow within your lifts, work, etc., and you figure out what is working, what is not working, and how to progress. This can be the same within machine learning, where the machine learns, grows, takes into account more data, information, etc., to perform the necessary outputs.

Supervised and unsupervised

Within machine learning, there are two areas of focus I want to address: supervised and unsupervised learning. Within the IBM article mentioned above, we learn that supervised learning "is defined by its use of labeled datasets to train algorithms that classify data or predict outcomes accurately." We can use the working out example again in this case. Supervised learning would be like going through a fitness regime with a personal trainer. The trainer helps you to learn and develop through your fitness goals. It is a "supervised" fitness program. This idea of supervised learning with machine learning works in the same way. There is a "supervisor" helping the learning go forward.

You may have guessed it, but unsupervised learning isn't going to have that "personal trainer" to help you through your fitness program. You go out, find the data, work through the data sets, and figure out how to best help your fitness and workout regime. From the IBM article we can think of unsupervised learning within machine learning as algorithms that study the data themselves and learn from within, "to analyze and cluster unlabeled datasets."

Deep learning

With machine learning, there is another area of data and analytics that has risen to prominence: deep learning. It is worth noting the difference between deep learning and machine. According to IBM (Cloud Education, 2020b), it's the way the algorithm learns that differentiates them. Deep learning is more "independent" of manual human interventions, automating a lot of the feature extraction processes and enabling the use of large data sets. With classical machine learning, human experts set the features needed to understand the differences between data inputs, so more structured data is often needed.

We can think of this in essence almost as if it were as supervised or human intervention-driven machine learning, and unsupervised, machine-driven machine learning.

The Cloud

In the growth and data-driven world, there is this nebulous area (funny that we can use the term nebulous within the world of the Cloud as we describe data) called "the Cloud." What is the Cloud? Where did it come from and how does it pertain to data?

By definition, "The Cloud refers to software and services that run on the internet, instead of locally on your computer" (Cha, 2015). In essence, the Cloud allows a user to access data and information, and allows you to run software and services that can be utilized anywhere you have an internet connection. This ability to access and run data and information anywhere is a critical and, let's face it, amazing feature for organizations to succeed.

Another feature of the Cloud within the world of data and analytics is the ability to store data cheaply. Historically, organizations may need to purchase servers and database software to store all of their data. Even in my time, the server used for data pulls and areas I was using in my world of data and analytics was stored in one of my boss's offices in New York City. This idea of storing a server in my boss's office is comical, as it would heat his office up, but shows that in the past the ability to store and use servers could be cumbersome or a tedious task, as an extra server was sitting in an office.

Overall, the Cloud offers us many features and abilities that enhance an organization's ability to utilize data and analytics, and to be truly data driven. If an organization is not investing in Cloud technology to enhance its ability to use data and be data driven, unfortunately that organization could find itself falling behind.

Databases

A database is an organized collection of structured information, or data, typically stored electronically in a computer system. A database is usually controlled by a database management system (DBMS). Together, the data and the DBMS, along with the applications that are associated with them, are referred to as a database system, often shortened to just database. (Oracle, 2021)

Databases are one of the most common types of data collection and storage within the industry. Organizations have been using databases for ages to collect the data and information needed to be a data-driven company. Unfortunately, just collecting the data hasn't been sufficient to achieve a data-driven organization; just collecting data isn't bringing insights to life, but rather just storing and collecting data. It takes more to bring it to life. Common database tools are (Forbes Technology Council, 2020):

- MySQL
- Oracle RDMS
- Salesforce
- DevOps
- Visual Studio Code

Again, this is not a full list of the tools and technology present in the world today. Databases are wonderful and powerful, but can be expensive and require different maintenance than the Cloud.

Data lakes

I want to share a story about this tool and technology, to help illuminate data lakes. I want you to imagine that you like fishing. For some of you, you may not have to imagine hard. You are heading to a lake to go fishing. This is a nice, natural lake with multiple rivers and creeks flowing into and out of it. You go to fish one day and have established what you think is the perfect bait, line, and rod to use to catch the fish. You are prepared to clean the fish afterwards and have great success there. Then, when ready, you set your bait on the fishing line, you stand up with the rod, you set the rod down, walk to the water's edge and hold out your arms and hands, hoping for the fish to jump into your waiting arms. Ummm, would that make you successful at fishing? Of course not! I do not know of one human being who has stood on the edge of a lake and fish jumped into their arms, although I am ready to be proven wrong. Data lakes are similar.

A data lake is a tool and technology where the rivers and creeks of data flow into it. It is a centralized repository in which can be stored both structured and unstructured data at any scale, and then run various analytics (from dashboards to big data processing) to guide better decision making (AWS Amazon, 2021).

In essence, a data lake is a tool and technology that allows for the unfiltered data to flow into it, driving what should be success, understanding, and a bunch of insight-driven approaches to data and analytics. So, why the fishing story above where the fish is not jumping into the arms of a fisherman any time soon? Because the insight is not going to jump into the arms of a data analyst or data scientist.

While on paper, a data lake seems like a wonderful investment for organizations to succeed, far too often data lakes have failed and not brought about the strong successful implementation that could come from having all your data, structured or unstructured, in the same place. Back in 2016, Gartner predicted that 60 percent of data lakes would fail. That number was revised to 85 percent just a year later (eWeek Editors, 2020). The article from 2020 that shared those metrics gives five areas organizations "must plan for in their data lake journey":

1 Chirping end-to-end orchestration of Cloud data lakes isn't easy.
2 Runaway costs and performance degradation occur with relentless monitoring and management.
3 Ensuring security, regulatory compliance, and governance can be tricky.
4 Hybrid architecture and multi-Cloud support is required.
5 Those who need the data need to be able to get it themselves.

This is a tall task for organizations. While the data lake seems like a wonderful proposition, the amount of work, time, and talent needed to drive it can be large. Here, we can see that just as a fish will NOT jump into your arms, a data insight is not just jumping out of a data lake for your success. The reality is, it will take specific skills within analytics (think the four levels) and then the ability to drive insight to action.

Human capital

Herein lies the final tool and technology I want to mention in this chapter: human capital. In order for organizations to be truly data driven, the most important tool they can purchase and utilize is human capital. There will be an estimated 11.5 million new jobs by 2026 (Cal University of Pennsylvania, 2021).

Throughout all the impact of data and technology, and their power, it is very apparent in organizations that in order for a company to truly be data driven and to succeed, they will need to have the right people in the right positions for the right work. This includes the need for data scientists, engineers working in AI and machine learning, data analysts working in business intelligence tools, and more. If a holistic strategy is put in place, organizations can succeed.

To understand the human capital piece of the tools and technology, it is important to understand how the data personas listed above interact with and are utilized throughout the puzzle that is a data-driven organization. In particular, for leadership in organizations, it is very important to understand the tools and technologies for the personas as it comes to the proper rollout of different tools and technologies in the organization. Doing this can help ensure the organization is ready to succeed through a personnel perspective.

Data scientist

It should come as no surprise that the data persona "data scientist" will utilize the different tools and technologies from the most advanced perspective. When we look at the list of the tools and technologies mentioned above, we can see that a data scientist will potentially use every single one of them. A flow-through could help to illuminate that.

A data scientist may utilize coding languages to build out code that will be populated and utilized by artificial intelligence and/or machine learning. When the artificial intelligence or machine learning gives results to the data scientist and end users of the platform, the data scientist can utilize the information for further analysis or to make a decision.

Another flow-through may be the more coding work that is done by the data scientist. The data scientist may use coding languages such as SQL, Python or R to gather data from the organization's database, Cloud, and/or data lake. This data can then be used through an analysis, such as with statistical testing, to decipher the insight within the information. Then, once the information is pulled, the data scientist can utilize a data visualization or business intelligence tool to find insight in the data to make a decision.

One thing to note within the world of data science and the work a data scientist is doing is that the majority of the time spent by data scientists is not in the analysis but in the cleansing and preparing of data. Instead of using their technical know-how to extract insight from the data, they spend their time cleaning it, losing that precious time and ability. This is a frustration among data scientists and a shame that their skill is not being utilized in a more effective manner. For leaders and everyone in an organization, having the right data strategy or outcome-based approach to data and analytics can help alleviate this frustration.

Data analyst

A data analyst will utilize data in a similar way to a data scientist, but we just want to scale back the advanced techniques or the technical skills that are required. Usually, the data analyst is spending more time within the world of business intelligence and data visualization than in the world of machine learning, artificial intelligence, coding, etc. This is not a bad thing, but it shows the extent to which the roles are present in the world today and how the technologies above are being utilized by different data personas.

It should be noted that data analysts do use coding languages such as SQL (probably the most common), R and Python. They can also use data lakes, databases and the Cloud. Once again, it should be the type of role and work being done that dictates which of these are being used.

Data engineer

A data engineer is really going to make themselves at home with the more advanced data storage technologies mentioned above and within the worlds of artificial intelligence and machine learning. From Coursera (2021) we learn that data engineering encompasses designing and building systems that collect, store and analyze data at scale. Data engineers can work in a variety of settings to build these systems that can turn raw data into usable information for people to interpret.

In other words, let's let the engineers do their jobs so the scientists and analysts can do theirs.

Business user

It is critical to understand just what a business user is in a data-driven culture and organization because they may be the key to unlocking an organization's true data-driven success. The vast majority of an organization will be made up of business users. Business users are those who aren't technical but will nonetheless still need to utilize data to make decisions. From a tools and technologies perspective, they will mainly be focused on the data visualization and business intelligence arena. This need and ability to work there comes from the fact that most of the people in the organization will not be technical or data scientists, but will still need to use data. Think of a marketing analyst or finance manager. Are they data engineers or scientists? No, they are not, but they still need to use data.

Think of an organization with 10,000 employees. The vast majority, probably upwards of 9,000, are not going to be analysts or scientists. Therefore, more likely, they are business users. They will use data visualization tools and techniques to bring data to life, to bring a data-driven organization to the forefront. Part of this solution necessitates the need for upskilling and data literacy.

Leadership

Leadership represents a unique spot in the world of data and analytical tools and technologies. Leaders most likely are not in the backend, messing around with the Cloud, databases, etc. Leaders are also not likely to be building the visualizations and techniques to bring an insight to life. The reality is, a leader will be the beneficiary of the results and insights shared with them. So, in essence, a leader is the recipient of the utilization of all the tools and technologies.

That said, the leader is also the one pulling the budget and spending power for those tools and technologies. This is a very important understanding to have. Leaders are not only making decisions as recipients of the information, they must lead the charge on where to invest and how to build the tool and technology stack to be used in data. This is why it is important to understand the technologies and tools, and to have a holistic strategy in place for their use.

Conclusion

We have spoken a lot about tools and technologies in this chapter. We have also briefly spoken about the roles that utilize those technologies. A quick repeat of those roles and technologies would be good to imprint within our minds. The roles we looked at were:

- data scientist
- data analyst
- data engineer
- business user
- leadership

The tools and technologies we examined were:

- business intelligence and data visualization
- data science
- coding languages

- artificial intelligence
- machine learning
- the Cloud
- databases
- data lakes
- human capital

All of these items mentioned above, both the data personas and the tools and technologies, are parts of the work to become truly data driven. In order for organizations to succeed with data and analytics and to be truly data driven, the organization must understand each of the data personas as well as the roles of the tools and technologies in the world today.

Far too often, organizations and leaders are impressed by a salesperson who can use a tuned-in data set, one that has been prepared for a scenario, and show how effective a tool can be. It is another thing when an organization takes that tool and tries to implement what they saw. Remember, start with your strategy and then let the tools and technologies fall into the hands of the right data personas. Doing this can help create more data-driven success.

4

What is a data-driven organization?

Within this book, we have covered the world of data today, and what the tools and technologies are within a data-driven organization. In this chapter, we want to bring it all together. In my years of working within data and analytics, and through watching what happened during the Covid-19 pandemic, I will use this chapter to illustrate the five key pillars that make up a data-driven organization, deliberately put in the order you see below:

- *Strategy*: What are we doing?
- *Leadership*: Who owns what we are doing?
- *Data literacy*: Do we have the skills to accomplish what we are doing?
- *Data and technology*: Do we have the data, access, and tools to drive data-driven decision making?
- *Culture*: Is the environment ready to succeed with data?

These five pillars are the key to a successful data-driven organization. The key may not be the pillars but the questions they solve, which are listed next to them. Through these questions, leaders and individuals can get past a nebulous understanding of the five pillars, so it is my hope that you will sit and look to answer them. Do you have a data strategy for your organization? What is leadership doing to help data and analytics succeed? What are the skills your organization has or does not have for success? What technology do you have and does it actually work for what you want to do? Finally, is your culture ready, and if not, how do you get there? Use this book to answer these questions on a consistent basis for yourself and your organization.

In this chapter we will cover three key areas:

- What is a data-driven organization?
- What are the five pillars?
- What are real-world examples of a data-driven organization in action?

This chapter will set the tone for individuals, organizations, and, most importantly, leadership to figure out just what a data-driven organization is. Please note that later in the book we will speak more on what holds organizations back from being truly data driven. This chapter is to allow the reader to understand the definition of being data driven, what the pillars are, and to offer examples. Use these three main areas to help define "data driven" and start to see what needs to be done within your organization.

What does data driven mean?

If "data driven" was one of the catchy phrases that really gathered momentum during the shutdowns and pandemic of Covid-19, what does it mean? A quick Google search could turn up many things, and the reality is that there are many definitions I like, but this is the one that most catches my eye:

> When a company employs a "data-driven" approach, it means it makes strategic decisions based on data analysis and interpretation. A data-driven approach enables companies to examine and organise their data with the goal of better serving their customers and consumers. (At Internet, 2021)

I might add, this is not just for their customers but for the overall improvement in many areas of business and the organization as a whole. Basically, a data-driven organization is one that utilizes data to improve its business—it is that simple. What are examples of data-driven organizations?

There are many examples, but the one I want to highlight right now with regards to a data-driven approach is the mega company: Amazon. Amazon has utilized data to help in its business for years. An *Entrepreneur* article listed a few characteristics of Jeff Bezos' approach to utilizing data and making Amazon into a data-driven organization (Selinger, 2014):

- metrics define your corporate culture
- listening to data starts at the top
- democratize data

I find that these three characteristics are key to being truly data driven. Let's dive into each.

Metric driven

Being metric driven should be a given, but is it truly how businesses operate? By definition, being metric driven is where an organization sets targets, metrics, measurable outputs within the organization that the workforce is trying to accomplish. Unfortunately, a lot of organizations are trying to be metric driven and they have a good start on it, but they can fall short. What is meant by "fall short" in this context is that organizations will set their KPIs and metrics, targets, and then report on those metrics and targets using descriptive analytics. From there… from there…. OK, this is where they fall short, by not providing diagnostic analytics and more.

Organizations are trying to be metric and KPI driven, but they lack the ability to do good insight-driven diagnostic analytics. They will build monthly and quarterly dashboards, running those through the teams and asking questions: "Why are we seeing this?" "What caused this influx here?" The problem is, without a data-literate workforce and data-driven organization, they will not use data to its full extent and allow it to empower the organization to answer those questions. They will try, but they will fall short.

Data starts at the top

The second notion we learn from Amazon and Jeff Bezos is that listening to data starts at the top. Data has to start at the top, as the leadership can set the tone for the rest of the organization. Within the leadership roles in an organization, you will usually find years of experience, but sometimes this experience gets in the way of listening to data. Please note, we are not stating that experience doesn't matter, because it plays a big part. Where the problem lies is when leaders listen to their gut and ignore the data. What we want to create is a balance between the human element and the data element.

If an organization sees its leaders working hard to listen to the data, combining it with other factors such as gut feel, the human element and experience, then the rest of the organization can buy into the notion that the organization wants to truly be data driven.

Democratizing data

The third piece of the puzzle provided by Amazon was democratizing data. To democratize data means to give it to the masses, the work-force and individuals. Amazon is right. For an organization to be data driven, it must put its data out to the masses. By giving it to the masses, you get more eyes on the data and information in front of them, and you potentially gain more insight. You can have different minds thinking on the information. I agree wholeheartedly that democratizing data and information is paramount to data-driven success, but please don't forget to ensure you have data literacy initiatives in the organization. If the organization is democratizing data and information to the masses but the masses aren't comfortable in using data, then the strategy can fall horribly short.

These three characteristics of a data-driven organization are correct and needed. We will now proceed to study and go through the different pillars I discovered over time that make up a data-driven organization: strategy, leadership, data literacy, data and technology, and culture.

The five pillars of a data-driven organization

Strategy

We all know what a strategy is, or at least I hope we do, but do we know what the formal definition is? From a business perspective, I like this one, included in the Management Study Guide (2021), which I will summarize here: that strategy is an action focused on attaining organizational goals—both present and future. It is also a general direction set for a company—a desired state in the future. Organizational resources are analyzed and allocated so as to meet these objectives.

Now, why is strategy a pillar for an organization that is looking to be data driven? Is it really a pillar? Let's be clear. In this case we are not talking about an organization's overarching strategy. We are speaking directly about a data strategy, which, without question, must be tied to the organization's overall strategy, its business strategy. If it isn't, I would ask, what are you doing?

Having a data strategy is paramount to success. As the definition above states, a data strategy would then be implied to be "an action managers take to attain one or more of the organization's goals" with data, and "a general direction set for the company and its various components to achieve a desired state in the future" by utilizing data and analytics. This must be a pillar for organizations to succeed as data driven. If the organization does not know where it is going with data and how data will be utilized to help the organization succeed, the overall work with data and analytics can be hindered. Let me share an example of an organization that had not facilitated throughout its workforce the company's overall data strategy, i.e., what did the company want to do with data?

I was meeting with a financial services firm that specialized in data. The individuals I was meeting with were discussing with me their data literacy learning strategy. They had built learning plans and how individuals could learn to use data more effectively in their roles. It was a good meeting, but there was one problem. I kept bringing up the question, "Do you know what your company is trying to do with data?" I asked this question multiple times and eventually the people I was meeting with understood: they should figure out what the organization was trying to do with data.

The reason this understanding was paramount to a data literacy success story was that if the learning program the team had built was not directed toward the company's goals and strategy with data, it might miss the mark on what the organization was trying to do. If the plan was rolled out, the team might have trained learners on data aspects in the arena of A, B, C, but in reality, the individuals needed to learn M, N, O. By not having a clear understanding of what the organization wanted to do, the plans could have been off by wide margins.

So what does a data strategy do to help shape an organization to be data driven? Here are just a few examples:

- A data engineer or data architect who is tasked with setting up the organization's data modeling will know where the company is going with data, thereby enabling this data engineer to build the right modeling for the strategy at hand. This will also help this employee shift the model if the leadership and organization deem a different direction is better.

- A data analyst who knows what the organization's data strategy is knows directions, questions, and insight to find that can help the organization succeed more in the strategy. In these instances, we are talking about a marketing analyst knowing how to pull data to help the latest campaign that was looking to fulfill one branch of the data strategy. A risk data analyst knows different levers to pull within the data and analytics they are working on, as the right lever can lead to success with the strategy at hand.

- A data scientist knows the modeling, coding, and other aspects needed to move toward sound predictive analytics that can help build predictions for different business units that are trying to move the organization forward toward strategic success.

Of course, these are just a few examples of employees who know what the data strategy is for the organization, AND know the outcomes and business strategy desired to help the organization succeed. An organizational data strategy is a starting point for an organization to succeed with being data driven. Figure out what exactly you want to do with data at your organization, then build a strategy to achieve that outcome, and your organization can be on its way to being data driven.

WHAT TO DO

Leadership must take the time and effort to either have the right leaders in place to drive the strategy or hire them. With the right strategy, organizations can succeed with data. If you do not have a data strategy, and by that I mean a holistic, company-wide data strategy, get one in place as soon as you can.

Leadership

The second pillar of a data-driven organization we want to discuss is leadership. This being said, we discussed a bit of this earlier in the chapter when defining a data-driven organization. In this section, I want to expand on that and truly drive home the importance of leadership in a data-driven organization.

In a study from Qlik (Qlik, 2021), it was found that only 24 percent of business decision makers and 32 percent of C-suite members found themselves confident in their data literacy skills. So, only one out of four business decision makers and one out of three in the C-suite. Now, data literacy is defined as the ability to read, work with, analyze, and argue or communicate with data (Qlik, 2021). If those are the numbers, then it is imperative that leadership become data literate themselves. If they are setting the data strategy, then we had better boost those numbers. But, leadership provides a key resource to the workforce.

Within a data-driven organization, leadership and its ability to take the organizational data strategy and bring it to light is crucial for an organization's data-driven success. First, leadership sets the tone for the organization and the organization will follow. In this case, if leadership is not using data and insight to make decisions, what incentive does an individual who is not comfortable using data have to use data to make decisions? If leadership gives budget and money to the organization to successfully implement data and analytical work, but doesn't invest much in the workforce as far as tooling and more, then will people buy into the catchy slogan they have used to get people excited to use data? One key component to a data-driven organization—and we will touch upon it in this chapter—is that leadership helps shape and set the tone for the culture of the organization.

One key area that may get overlooked in organizations regarding leadership and its ability to build and successfully implement a data-driven organization is that leadership is in charge of hiring, retention, upskilling, and reskilling. As leadership looks to build a successful company or organization, and as the organization looks to be data driven, hiring the right personnel is crucial for success. If leadership has bought into the data strategy and is all in on being data driven, then hiring the right personnel and employees is key. Leadership should know what skills to look for, what soft skills complement the technical, and they should know how the employees fit into the data strategy. This also involves the retention of employees, especially when it comes to corrections and areas of improvement to ensure employee retention. It also helps set the stage and tone for upskilling and reskilling initiatives, which are necessary for organizations to succeed with data.

Leadership is essential for a data-driven organization, this is true. It is also true that leadership doesn't need to know everything when it comes to data, but must ensure they are confident in their data literacy skills to ensure the right strategy, culture, etc. are in place for success.

WHAT TO DO

As leadership, ensure you yourself are strong in your data literacy skills. Second, ensure your leadership team is. Third, ensure your workforce is. Along with these areas of focus, ensure you are set with the right leadership structure around data. Ensure everyone is on board, strong, and knowledgeable. Finally, lead your team and the company to truly be data driven. The culture side is something you can influence heavily, so do so and help people want to use the power of data.

Data literacy

Data literacy is a key element throughout any data-driven organization because within data literacy is found the human element. As defined above, data literacy is the ability to read, work with, analyze, and argue or communicate with data. There are four key characteristics for us to know and learn, and we will cover each one in short detail, but first, notice what is missing from the definition of data literacy: data science. Not everyone in the world needs to be a data scientist, but all need to be data literate. Now, in this case, data literacy can be an all-encompassing area wherein lie all data skills. In my first book, *Be Data Literate*, I discuss this topic at length, so we will not discuss data literacy ad nauseam. Instead, we will touch upon the key elements that make it up and how it can help an organization flow with its data-driven success.

The first characteristic is the ability to read data. This is the ability of individuals in a workforce to have confidence that when presented with data, they have the ability to read and comprehend what they are looking at. The ability to read data is probably the most essential characteristic in the definition because if you cannot read data, how will you work with, analyze, or argue and communicate with it? The ability to read will also vary across individuals in the organization. If you are a data scientist, you will be reading more complex models, code, and/or analysis. If you are a beginner or end user, you might only be looking at the end product of a dashboard or data visualization. These varying skills are important to understanding how a data-driven organization works and how the pieces flow through together and appropriately.

The second characteristic is the ability to work with data. Just like the ability to read data effectively, the ability to work with data will have varying skills across the board. End users may just be picking up the PowerPoint presentation with the charts attached and then reading through them. A data analyst may be gathering the data, sourcing it, and then building a data visualization to map the latest marketing campaign against specific targets. Finally, a machine learning engineer may be mapping code, working with the models, to ensure the machine learning capabilities and operations are in harmony with the data strategy that has been set forth. Overall, these different areas of working with data are crucial elements to a data-driven organization.

The third characteristic is the ability to analyze data. Within analyzing data we are brought the four levels of analytics: descriptive, diagnostic, predictive, and prescriptive. We will not exhaust that list in this book, but each of these types of analytics has a role within the organization's data strategy. As a part of the characteristics of data literacy, analyzing data is how we find insight. It is the ability to ask good questions, apply the human element against your analysis, and use these techniques to find insight for a decision in an organization. That is the ability to analyze data.

The final characteristic is the ability to argue and/or communicate with data. This is a soft skill: the ability to communicate effectively. I want you to imagine this. You were a part of a data project that built a strong analysis and model to help make a crucial product launch decision. The analysis is sound, is double-checked, and then checked again. Then, as you get the chance to present the information, you find that no one knows how to articulate the analysis and insight to different teams in order to make a decision. This may seem ridiculous, but it is just an example of how organizations can be frustrated in their data-driven work as people cannot communicate analysis or results effectively.

Overall, data literacy is a key pillar and strength for the organization. As part of the five pillars of a data-driven strategy, data literacy helps implement a data strategy with success. Leadership, the second pillar, will be the ones who put a data literacy learning strategy in place. By understanding the make-up of the workforce and the need for upskilling and reskilling, leadership can help ensure data literacy permeates through the organization's framework and workforce.

WHAT TO DO

As leaders and individuals, drive a data literacy initiative personally with yourself to begin, but then lead it in your team, business unit, and/or organization. These things are key to driving success. Data literacy is a wonderful way for an organization to ensure data and analytical success, and to build a truly data-driven organization.

Data and technology

Historically, organizations would do a certain thing, which they shouldn't have, as their data strategy: they would buy a data tool, such as Tableau or Qlik, and call it a strategy. Let's make one thing very clear upfront: a tool is not a strategy. It is a tool. It is found in its name. Now, that being said, data and technology play an amazing role in the pillars of a data-driven organization.

First, let's talk about the data itself. With the prevalence of so many data-producing devices, data is being created in record amounts. What seemed like a lot years ago is now only a blip on our data-producing radar. Now, this data is not being fully utilized. Back in 2012, only 0.5 percent of data was being analyzed (Petrov, 2021). If we look at just how much data is being produced, and at that time we were only analyzing 0.5 percent of data, we can see that a huge gap exists. With technology, data literacy, etc., all of these pieces come together.

With data come many different areas to think through: ethics, regulation, governance, cleansing of the data, democratization, all of it. Data doesn't just come to an organization ready-made for our use, there are other factors that need to be in place to ensure the data is ready for use and sound. In can step the other world of technology.

Technology represents so much, and we have discussed much of it in the previous chapter. Within technology, we have tools that allow the democratization of data to the masses. We find the ability to store large quantities of data in the Cloud. We have data scientists and engineers using coding to put in place advanced analyses or models. Technology is not only a key element, but the adaptation of the data and technology to the needs of the organization helps an organization be flexible and adapt to the changing environment around them.

With the other characteristics already mentioned, how do the first three pillars interact with this fourth pillar? As a part of the organization's data strategy, included should be what tools and technology the company wants to invest in to ensure a successful strategic implementation. You can't give a person a screwdriver to cut the wood for the house you are building, but give them a saw and watch the success roll. Then, when the strategy is in place for what tools and technologies will be purchased and utilized, leaders pull the trigger on budget, investment, training, and usage of the tools and technology. Finally, data literacy can then empower the individual users to use the tools correctly and soundly. With the right data literacy skills, the data can come to life through the technology.

WHAT TO DO

Invest in the right data and technology. Let your data strategy help drive this for you. The strategy sets the tone for what you are doing and what you are looking to accomplish. Use that strategy to then dictate the right software and technology for you, not a fancy salesperson who knows how to make a technology shine.

Culture

When I am asked what the number one roadblock is to data and analytical success, and in this case we can add in a data-driven organization, unequivocally the answer is the culture of the organization. Some may say data quality, data trustworthiness, the tools they have, availability of data, lack of skills, but they would all be wrong. The main roadblock to data and analytical success is the culture of the organization. How could this be? How could culture affect data and analytical work so much? Before answering these questions, let me define what I mean by an organizational culture.

The culture of an organization as I define it can be broken down to four legs of a stool: 1) the traditions, or heuristics, at the organization; 2) the skill set of the organization; 3) the beliefs of the organization; and 4) the organization's personality and/or way of doing things. With this four-legged stool, one can see stability, how an organization flows, especially with the personality of the organization. Within my career, I see how these pillars of an organizational culture flow through the people and work done for success. I can also view how this culture can hinder or help the flow of data and analytics throughout. Let me explain through my personal history.

Early in my career, I worked in a group that was very talented with descriptive analytics. This was a great boost for me as I started off my career, but looking back, while the group was good at descriptive analytics, the ability to dive deeper or make changes was lacking. When one wanted to change a report or dashboard, it was met with hesitancy, resistance, etc., causing the flow of data evolution or other things to be stymied. This is not a strong, conducive way to be data driven.

At another point in my career, when working with an organization that was strong with data and analytics, the culture was ripe for success but slow moving. I distinctly remember having a conversation where one of the executives of the company told me the new way he was having his team work with data. No longer would one of their team meetings be the team walking through the dashboard they had built. Instead, the dashboard needed to be done in advance, and he would then review it. The team was now positioned and told they needed to come to the meeting ready to speak to what was within the dashboard, not just walk through it. This was a cultural shift for one team, but the meetings became more effective. The meetings became about the "why" and not just the "what." This type of cultural work is essential.

Finally, in the last example of my career, in working with organizations all over the world I have noticed that there is a sense of the need to follow along and do all the "buzzwords"… and I say "do" very loosely here. Instead of "doing" them or accomplishing them, many companies like to march around and use the buzzwords to describe their work within data and analytics. Unfortunately, most of these organizations fall short of actually accomplishing what the buzzword is intending. For example, when companies and employees consistently say they are "data driven" I can cringe but have optimism. Unfortunately, what I usually see is the company pulling in lots of data and producing a lot of data, dashboards, etc., but when it comes to the effectiveness of these organizations to push through and succeed with data-driven decision making and a powerful use of data, they fall short. This does not come from lack of trying, but comes from lack of skills, a culture not ready to absorb true data work, etc.

One may ask oneself: these are great examples, but why is culture the number one roadblock to succeeding as a data-driven organization? Think of the stool analogy that was presented above. With these four pillars—traditions, skills, beliefs, and personality—if one of the legs of the stool is not strong or ready and willing to accept data work, the stool becomes wobbly and can fall. For organizations to be truly successful with data and analytics, these four legs need to be strong and steady, ready to use data to drive successful work. If the skills are not strong within the organization, data work can falter. If the beliefs of the organization do not coincide with a belief that data matters, the organization can falter as a data-driven organization. If the personality believes more in gut feel and not in the power of data, the organization can falter.

Overall, one can see how the culture of the organization ebbs, flows, and influences the ability to be data driven. Never underestimate the impact of an organization being ready to actually use data. Far too often, I am afraid, organizations get ahead of themselves and buy all the storage capacity, tools, technology, etc. to use data but fail to become data driven because they were not prepared for the cultural impact to take effect.

WHAT TO DO

Ensure your culture is ready to succeed. Look at the pillars that exist within the data-driven culture. What areas need improvement? Are people ready to drive data-driven success? Do you have sound change management principles in place to help this all work? If you can't answer these questions in a strong and satisfactory way, then it is time to really home in on your culture. Without that knowledge and capability, you might see all your goals and dreams of being data driven fade away.

Data-driven organizations in action

Now that we have described the five pillars, let us take a look at real-world examples of data-driven organizations, what they are doing to be successful, and use this as an opportunity to provide tips and training for how you and your organization can be successful.

EXAMPLE 1

Starbucks

How many of us like a fresh cup of coffee? How many of us like it or feel good when an organization or business truly knows us and customizes things for us? I know I like it and feel the personal touch when a company knows my order. Starbucks is in the customer service industry, not necessarily in the coffee and beverage business. In an article for Kolabtree, Nathan Sykes shares that the mobile app is a great driver for Starbucks and its use of data.

Many of the customers who order drinks utilize the Starbucks app itself to do so. While an individual utilizes the app, Starbucks also benefits, by gathering data, looking at patterns, trends, and more. With this data and information, Starbucks can customize and make recommendations to you. At the same time, it can utilize the data to help with targeted campaigns for customers, marketing campaigns, and more. Starbucks is utilizing data to be data driven. Again, Starbucks is not in the beverage industry, it is in the customer service industry. By targeting better, learning and understanding its customers, the company is driving a data-driven approach to its business.

Within this example, we can see that Starbucks has the data, technology, strategy, and leadership to deploy its data-driven strategy.

SOURCE Sykes (2018)

EXAMPLE 2

Airbnb

I love the example of using data that is Airbnb. The business model of Airbnb is fascinating and provides a treasure trove of data. Through Annex Cloud, we get a taste of what Airbnb is able to do through a data-driven approach.

Airbnb is able to offer personalized experiences and concierge by getting to know its customers more and more. To me, again, Airbnb is not in the business of vacation rentals, it is in the business of customer service.

As we continue to drive forward in the digital world, many of us don't want to talk on the phone much. Instead, we would like to utilize our technology to make decisions. Airbnb and concierge services are no different. Through the use of the app, website, etc., Airbnb is able to collect data and information on its users. As those users are using more and more technology, Airbnb can use that data to personalize the concierge services that are offered through its different digital channels, helping users to make decisions on what they would like to do when they travel, where to stay, places to visit, etc. As one who loves to travel the world, the ability to have a more personalized approach to my travel needs is something I desire.

Now, one thing to note: Airbnb is providing me, from a personal perspective, information that I can then use individually in a data-driven decision. Isn't that interesting? Airbnb is collecting my data and information to drive better data-driven decisions within its platform.

SOURCE Price (2021)

EXAMPLE 3
PepsiCo

During the Covid-19 pandemic, it is no secret that supply chains were hampered and affected greatly by economies and businesses shutting down, workforces needing to be furloughed, etc. This caused a large issue throughout the world, with businesses and individuals needing supplies and other things. In the case of PepsiCo, it has been using data for its supply chain since before the pandemic. Herein we see a business that had a data model for supply chains previously that could help it during this time.

To help ensure PepsiCo maintains its supply chain correctly, it uses volumes of data to help drive and ensure its retailers have the right products, at the right time, in the right amount. What is very interesting in all of this is there are examples of organizations, one in particular comes to mind, where the right amount of product, volume, etc. was not used correctly. This was one of the largest retailers in the United States and it is no longer in business.

SOURCE Kopanakis (2021)

EXAMPLE 4

Flatiron Health and cancer

It is no secret that the healthcare industry is ripe for the use of data. Through the pandemic, we individually saw data points each and every day on what was happening. In fact, it is predicted that the big data analytics market in healthcare will reach US $101 billion by the year 2031 (Visiongain LTD, 2021). Which company doesn't want a piece of that pie?

That being said, I want to focus this example on one organization using data to improve and help with its care of cancer: Flatiron Health. Flatiron Health "utilizes billions of data points from cancer patients to enhance research and gain new insights for patient care. Their solutions connect all players in the treatment of cancer, from oncologists and hospitals to academics and life science researchers, enabling them to learn from each patient."

This ability to use data to improve the care of those who are going through a challenge, such as cancer, the ability to improve care, gain insights, and connect different players in the sphere of cancer treatment and prevention, is fantastic.

SOURCE Schroer (2019)

Conclusion

We have seen the world of data accelerating for years. The Covid-19 pandemic set in motion more speed for individuals and organizations to truly be data driven. Through the pandemic, I found five pillars that drive and establish a data-driven organization. As a reminder, those are:

- **Strategy:** What are we doing?
- **Leadership:** Who owns what we are doing?
- **Data literacy:** Do we have the skills to accomplish what we are doing?

- **Data and technology:** Do we have the data, access, and tools to drive data-driven decision making?
- **Culture:** Is the environment ready to succeed with data?

Through these five pillars, an organization can be more successful with being data driven. Without them, an organization can be steering a boat blindly, not sure how to navigate the storms and issues that are coming in the future. The key is for organizational leadership to make the right investments in time, energy, talent, and strategy. To do this correctly, leadership need to ensure they are in place to drive each of these areas correctly.

PART TWO

Gaps

In this section, we will uncover gaps that cause issues for organizations to be truly data driven.

5

Foundational skills gaps

Skills gap:

> a fundamental mismatch between the skills that employers rely
> upon in their employees, and the skills that job seekers possess.
> This mismatch makes it difficult for individuals to find jobs and for
> employers to find appropriately trained workers. (Levesque, 2019)

As organizations have tried to be "data driven," with a heavy emphasis on the quotation marks here, there is one area that seems to be the focus: the tools and technology. Now, we have spoken a lot about tools and technology in this book, and this is ok—they play an important part. That is just it, though. Tools and technology from the world of being data driven are enablers—they are not the overall solution. Let me share an example of an organization that was doing what many others were doing within the world of data and analytics. This organization was blaming the tool for its poor data and analytical adoption.

I was working in my role of data literacy when a sales rep for the company reached out to me. There was a large financial institution in Australia that was not satisfied or happy with the adoption rate of the data and analytical tool that they were using. The type of tool was a business intelligence tool, like Tableau, Qlik, or Power BI. The organization felt they were getting about a 30 percent adoption rate for the tool they had purchased. With that low adoption rate, the team had requested that our company give them a request for proposal on the tool, but they were also going to be shopping elsewhere with another tool or two. A request for proposal means they were looking for a tool to replace the one they had purchased. Doing this new request to shop and see what else is out there can be significant. Time and energy have been spent with the old tool and would be required with the new tool. With that backdrop, the sales rep reached out to me to see what I suggested. Herein came my experience and background.

This organization was doing what other organizations do, and this is a trend that can be found all over the world: they blamed the technology for the poor adoption rates within the investments in data and analytics. They felt that the tool was the problem. As I spoke to the sales rep, it was my job to help craft the story to help our sales team to build the right narrative around the tool. Like with other companies, and I use this example often, requesting that different tools and technologies make proposals and bids is not going to be effective, not at all. Why? Why would talking about tools and technologies not be effective? The reason is that the tool and technology are not to blame. The data literacy skills gap is.

In this case, if this organization has had this discussion around the tool, looking for others to bid so they can finally get "adoption" because they have a new tool will not lead to success. My comment to this day is that the organization would be back at this, doing another request for proposal in 12 months. The key is not to drive a request for proposal, getting another tool in place that the employees would still not use. This would actually hamper the speed at which the organization becomes data driven. Instead, the key is to help the employees focus on knowing how to use data itself, how to use the four levels of analytics, and in turn, the tool can be just that, a tool for success.

This trend is one you can see over and over. Organizations are enamored with the latest tool and technology, being shown powerful demos that absolutely make the business intelligence or data science tool work like a charm, magically producing beautiful visualizations and pictures of the data in front of them. This could make it easy to say: "Wow, this is powerful, we need this tool." Then, as organizations put in place this powerful tool, they find it isn't going as smoothly, the data and pictures the tool brings to light aren't as effective, it isn't as easy, and more time and cost are thrown into the equation. Before you know it, you hate the tool and want to find a new one. All the while, the issues were not the tool or technology itself but the skills gaps that exist. What skills gaps exist? There are multiple. This chapter is dedicated to the skills gaps that exist in data and analytics, why they matter to a data-driven organization, and what can be done to solve them. Please note: this chapter will focus on data literacy and the technical skills gaps. Subsequent chapters will focus on holes in data strategy, leadership, and culture.

Fundamental skills gap: data literacy

In my work, there is a common theme I see over and over again: organizations are wanting data literacy and to improve the overall data and analytical skills within their organizations. To understand why they want data literacy initiatives, it will help us to understand what data literacy is, what the skills gap is within data literacy, and what solving the data literacy skills gap can do for organizations. To begin, let us define data literacy and understand its different characteristics.

Please note, we will not be doing a long treatise on the world of data literacy—that was done in my first book, *Be Data Literate: The data literacy skills everyone needs to succeed*. We have also provided a definition of data literacy in the context of a data-driven organization in the previous chapter. Herein, we will give a concise summary, but a shorter narrative nonetheless.

Data literacy

Definitions of data literacy often cite the ability to read, analyze and communicate with data. Both Panetta (2021) and Qlik (2021) also note that it empowers and encourages employees in their ability to use technology, make decisions and therefore drive effective business outcomes.

Data literacy is a fundamental ability to use data effectively. Does this mean that you have to learn the technical trades and skills to become a data scientist? No, of course not. Also, do you see the words "data science" within the definitions above? No, you don't. The reality is, data literacy is an essential and foundational skill that is needed across organizations to ensure data and analytical success. But what is the skills gap that exists within data literacy and how does this impact an organization trying to be data driven? Let's take a look at multiple studies that have been conducted that illuminate the skills gap, then we will discuss how solving this gap is vital to an organization being data driven.

The data literacy skills gap

In a study conducted by Qlik, it was found that "In a recent Censuswide survey done on behalf of Qlik, more than 7,300 business decision makers, just 24%, consider themselves data literate." Also, it was found that "Despite 92% of business decision makers believing it is important for their employees to be data literate, only 17% report that their business significantly encourages employees to become more confident with data" (Qlik, 2021). The great data spokesperson and influencer, Bernard Marr, said, "The more empowered employees are to read, write, analyze and argue with data, the more they will be able to contribute to their roles and the future of their organizations" (Qlik, 2021). What do these quotes mean? What kind of impact does this have on an individual, leadership, and an organization as a whole?

To begin, these skills gaps represent a widening gap in the ability of leadership to help its organization become data driven. As leaders are investing in their organizations to be data driven, buying the right technology and software, looking at hiring the right people, and so forth, this skills gap in data literacy becomes a large impedance for data-driven success. By having a data literacy gap within the organization, meaning a lack of ability to read, work with, analyze, and communicate with data, the organization is losing out on key capabilities to help it utilize data to improve operations and make decisions.

One of the key aspects in the quote above is the lack of decision makers getting behind their organizations and workforces for upskilling and reskilling around data and analytics. This goes back to an old saying: "The road to hell is paved with good intentions."

Organizationally, a fundamental gap exists between the desire to utilize data more effectively (I believe many, if not all, organizations know data is here and is now or will be part of the future of work) and the skills to do so. Why do we not see a greater push than 17 percent of decision makers significantly encouraging employees to become more confident with data, especially if 92 percent believe it is important to be data literate? That is quite the paradox we can see. Again, we can't just talk the talk, we do need to greatly encourage and help people and organizations to walk the walk. If you are a leader, start to own this data literacy gap and your ability to close it. Start to own the investment in your people, with time, technology, and learning that prepares them to truly be data driven. Start to own the strategy. If you aren't a leader, be a leader without the title. Set the example, own your own data literacy strategy. Build your skills and abilities. Make yourself more marketable to your organization. With this new and relevant information, what value does data literacy bring to an organization?

How data literacy can benefit an organization

At first glance, it would appear that if leadership were to put in place a data literacy initiative there would be fundamental shifts and changes to an organization's ability to succeed with data. Data literacy empowers employees to make smarter, data-driven decisions. By making smarter decisions with data, we start to see an organization utilize data for its purpose.

Empowerment

First, one value that data literacy brings is the empowerment of the workforce. In my work, I have been asked multiple times to teach

Human Resources groups about the value and power of data and data literacy. In these discussions, with a more data-literate workforce within the Human Resources groups at an organization, there are multiple benefits that an organization can experience as part of a strategy to become data driven, including the following.

HIRING IMPROVEMENT

With a data-literate workforce within Human Resources, the hiring practices can be improved. With data literacy, there is greater ability to know what to look for within candidates, which skills are proving most valuable for positions within your company, etc. Data literacy helps build a data-driven organization through hiring practices.

DEVELOPMENT AND RETENTION

Within an organization, the attrition of employees, the development programs, benefits, bonuses, etc. can be improved by understanding markets, trends, and more. By understanding how to read, work with, and analyze data, individuals can find the key insights and data points that may help them hire and retain employees better.

Marketing

Another area where data literacy can help an organization to be data driven is through its marketing department. Marketing departments have worked for years to use data, information, and other points to help inform them within their work. Part of that work has been based off the human "gut instinct" and their personal thoughts that will help marketing to be more successful. Within this world of data and analytics, the ability to understand trends and information can be paramount for marketing success. Here are ways data literacy will help marketing employees to be more data driven.

TARGETING

Using data and information to figure out which customers to target is not new and has been around forever, but how many individuals in marketing are used to truly using data and analytics to find insight? With data literacy, that ability to work with and analyze the data to find the insight for a marketing campaign will help the marketing teams to drive more success with its targeting goals.

CAMPAIGN ANALYSIS

Using data and information, marketing teams around the world can understand and analyze the marketing campaigns they are a part of more effectively. We tend to think of using data in marketing to analyze how to target better, as mentioned above. In this case, using data literacy skills to understand, analyze, and then communicate out the analysis of a marketing campaign and its performance can truly enhance an organization's data-driven abilities. In this case, as we look at analyzing a marketing campaign to understand if it was successful or not, having a strong data-driven culture and data-literate skill set throughout the workforce, the company can use all four levels of analytics (descriptive, diagnostic, predictive, and prescriptive) to analyze the campaign effectively. Let's look at the four levels of analytics and data literacy skills, and how closing the skills gap can drive an effective data driven-culture and solution.

Descriptive analytics   Using data literacy skills, individuals who are working to analyze the campaign performance will be able to describe the data and information as it comes in on the campaign, and post-campaign for overall performance. "The campaign drove x, y, and z," or "Through the campaign, we were able to build this dashboard that shows a, b, and c."

Diagnostic analytics   Using the descriptive analytics, the data-literate workforce can then diagnose what happened through the campaign, diving in and understanding the "why" behind the numbers themselves. This skill set of data literacy that permeates throughout the marketing organization is vital for the true understanding of what happened through the marketing campaign. This ability to truly understand and find the "why" behind the movement of customers, demographics, etc. is a key to truly being data driven.

Predictive analytics   Once the marketing team has used its data literacy skills to find the "why" behind the numbers and movement, we can then use data literacy skills and partner with the more technical group of data scientists, if the marketing group does not have this skill set, and form hypotheses to drive conclusions: "We saw this in the marketing campaigns and we learned why this is. Let's build predictions around this why to help us find more success." These predictions can then themselves gather data. With that data, new descriptive analytics can be built and diagnostic analytics used to find the insight and why through the numbers. Thus, the iterative process of data and analytics is unfolding and an organization can utilize this rolling process to be data driven. A side note here: a lot of times I see data and analytical work as "one-off projects" or the like. This can be effective in some cases and can help organizations to have some success, but the reality is a more holistic, strategic approach to data and analytics is more effective and desired. This approach flows through the whole organization and is tied back to the business strategy. This is of paramount importance because the workforce then can find the base and foundation to the data work and it isn't haphazard, sporadic work. This more focused approach should lead you to more adoption of data and analytics.

Prescriptive analytics   Sometimes, as an organization becomes more and more data driven, the use of "external means" to drive solutions can come into place. Back in marketing, as the team is more data driven, as the organization has worked to build out solutions, it has invested in tools and technologies that can simplify or make life easier for the marketers as they are working through their thoughts and solutions. In this case, the tool is building out prescriptive analytics— think of machine learning and artificial intelligence. These prescriptive analytics are there and designed to help facilitate what the marketing team should do in its work. Here, a data-literate workforce is still necessary to help the marketing team and organization's success because as the machine learning and artificial intelligence tools share information to the team, the team must be able to read, work with, analyze, and communicate the results.

Overall, the data literacy skills gap is one that, if closed properly, should see organizations achieve greater success within data and analytics. Unfortunately, data and analytical adoption is not where it should be. Gartner reports that "more than 87% of businesses were classified as having low business intelligence (BI) and analytics maturity" and "just 27% of businesses in 2020 consider their work environment to be 'data-driven'" (Impact, 2021). This lower adoption rate, maturity rate, etc. should be quite concerning to organizations that are investing and spending large sums of money on data and analytical tools, technologies, and the like. In this case, imagine if you were to raise your adoption rate. Imagine if your organization found itself building out a data literacy initiative to upskill and reskill your workforce. You discovered that like the Qlik study, only 20 percent of your workforce, or one in five, found themselves confident in using data. Now imagine if you can increase your organization's data literacy skills to make 40 or 50 percent of the workforce confident. Why did I stop at 40 or 50 percent and not go higher? Because it is a process. Of course we want to see the workforce data literacy confidence higher than that, and it can and will be if a proper data literacy strategy goes into place. We also know that the process takes time. There is also maybe another thought on your mind, one that can sit within leadership heavily: what kind of value does data literacy bring to my organization? Or does it bring any value? I hear about data literacy all the time: does it actually do or mean anything to my organization?

The answer to these questions is an unequivocal "yes" and that there is immense value to having data literacy in your organization. One of the best things is, especially considering the title and purpose of this book, that having a more data-literate organization can help both your organization and personal career to be more data driven.

The value of data literacy in being a data-driven organization

One key question can be asked: if we improve our data literacy, what value will we receive? What does having a data-literate workforce do for my organization? How does a data-literate workforce help us to be a data-driven organization? These questions are important ones that every individual in an organization should ask, especially leadership. Leaders are consistently saying they want to be data driven, that they want to use data more effectively to make decisions and drive the business, but the proper investment needs to be made to close this very important skills gap. To help us understand some of the value that comes from having a data-literate workforce, let's turn to a study I was able to participate in during my career.

Through this study, called the Data Literacy Index, commissioned by Qlik on behalf of the Data Literacy Project, in partnership with IHS Markit, PSB Research, and academics from the Wharton School, University of Pennsylvania, it was found that there was strong, true value in being a top-tier data-literate organization (The Data Literacy Project, 2021). The study created pillars of corporate data literacy. Organizations were ranked in the degree to which they displayed these pillars. Those pillars are:

- **Data literacy (human capital skills):** the skills of the organization
- **Data-driven decision making:** data decentralization and data resources
- **Data dispersion:** the widespread use of data throughout an organization.

This study showed significant findings as to the power of data literacy and its effect on organizations.

Organizations that ranked in the top third of the Data Literacy Index were associated with a 3–5 percent greater enterprise value (market capitalization). This doesn't mean much without context. For the organizations that participated in the study, this meant around $320–$534 million. The average organization size in the study was $10.7 billion.

Along with these numbers, it was found that improved data literacy positively impacts other measures of corporate performance as well, including gross margin, return-on-assets, return-on-equity, and return-on-sales.

Looking at these improved metrics, which organization and leader doesn't want improved gross margin, return-on-assets, return-on-equity, and return-on-sales? To me, this is one of the essences of a data-driven organization, one where the target metrics and desired metrics are improved.

To understand this and its impact on a data-driven organization, it is important to understand again that being data driven means we are using data to help the organization make decisions, improve operations, and so forth. With regards to data literacy, we can see the great impact and influence it can have on the organization being successfully data driven. Leaders in each and every organization should put forth the effort to drive a data literacy initiative to help drive a data-driven approach to work. The next question can become: how can we drive a data literacy initiative in our organization?

Building a data-literate workforce: a strategy

To help bring to life a data-literate workforce, organizations can follow certain steps and programs to help drive a successful data literacy initiative of upskilling and reskilling. As I list the steps to do this, please note that this is not a one-size-fits-all approach to building data literacy. What I will share is a good backbone or skeleton to how you and your organization can build data literacy to be a data-driven organization. These program pieces are as follows:

- assess your workforce
- communication plans
- persona-based learning programs
- cohort approach to learning
- metrics and measurement
- iterative approach

Let's evaluate each one on its own, but with an understanding that they all tie together to create a holistic approach to data literacy.

Assess your workforce

Take a quick moment to think about yourself, your team, the people you know, and/or your organization: how many of you went to school or have an educational background in a field that was specific to using data and analytics? The answer to that question is usually few. I remember a specific story where I was speaking at a big data and analytics conference in healthcare. As I addressed the audience, I asked them that question: how many of you studied for a background in data and analytics? Now, remember, this is a data and analytics conference. As I scanned the room for raised hands, I maybe saw around 40 out of a room of 200—maybe 20 to 30 percent. The reality is, not many have studied for and acquired a background in data. Now, full disclosure, we are starting to see that number increase. We are seeing more and more people study for a background in the STEM or STEAM fields: science, technology, engineering, arts, and mathematics. But with so few currently having this background in the field of data and analytics, we see more transparently why a data literacy initiative could be impactful and why being data driven has usually fallen short.

With the knowledge of the lack of skills and backgrounds in these fields, we can jump to the first thing an organization should do within a data literacy initiative: assess the individuals within the initiative. The world of data and analytics is vast and expansive. There are many different jobs and roles within this world. If an organization were to take a training program that had all the same curriculum and background, same courses, same content, and give every single employee this content, the program would fall short. Why? Because of the varying backgrounds and skill sets that the organization will have within data and analytics. Some will be technical, such as data scientists or data engineers; some will have no background in these fields whatsoever and if the program is technical, they can be lost very early on—and there are many other variations.

This one-size-does-NOT-fit-all approach is the best way to drive a data literacy initiative. Have each individual who is going to participate take an assessment to see where they are with their skills and comfort level in data and analytics. There can be various assessments given to the employees. If a person has a title of "data scientist" or "data engineer" we know a basic assessment is not going to be the most effective way for them to approach the topic at hand. Use varying assessments to define or illuminate where the person's current skills reside. Once this is known, we can then set them out on a prescribed learning path based on the results.

From here, the assessments become a crucial step one. This sets the tone, letting the learners and individuals know this will not be a "mandatory"-type training program, but one more specified to their needs. The assessments also help an organization map out the "lay of the land" for understanding what the organization looks like from a skills position. Having your organization map out its skills through these assessments can then help in understanding where its gaps may be, where the talent resides, how to create a more effective and holistic approach to data, etc. This assessment work can lay out a strong understanding and foundation for knowledge on your organization. This understanding of the talent you have can help you become more data driven, especially as it shows the gaps, potentially influencing your hiring of positions, who you can turn to, and potentially how to influence your culture.

Communication plans

Let me start this section by asking you a quick question: Do you like receiving an email that says you have mandatory training? No? You don't like getting those emails in the middle of your day that tell you you have to complete training by a certain day? No, most of us don't enjoy those emails. In fact, if you are like me you groan and think, "How can I get this done quickly?" A lot of people just click through and hit the button that says I accomplished this training. Of course this is not effective. If we were to build out these data literacy training programs and just say "you have a mandatory assessment to take," it could lose a drastic amount of effectiveness for your organization's data literacy initiative.

Instead of an email that goes out and tells individuals what they have to do, I work with organizations and discuss the need for a strong communication plan to correspond with the data literacy initiative. What do I mean by a strong communication plan? Isn't an email that says they have mandatory training a communication that is sent out from the initiative to the team members who will participate? Yes, it is a communication, but it is a weak and bare minimum communication.

When we formulate our holistic approach to data literacy learning, we want to have buy-in from the people who will be participating in the program. We need to establish the "why" before we get the learners in the program and learning. We can do this through email communication and setting up webinars to help the learners understand why the organization is taking on this new initiative. We can set the tone so the learners have a firm grasp of why the organization is taking on this initiative, what it means for them as learners, how data literacy can benefit them and the organization, and "what" and "how" the program will unfold. Doing this can help the learner understand the program, its purpose, their role in it, and set a foundation for the program's success.

Persona-based learning

The world of data and analytics in an organization is based upon data personas or personalities. You may be asking yourself, "What is a data persona?" A data persona can be broken down into the roles and uses of data an individual has within data and analytics. In this case, let's share the breakdown by the individual's roles within the organization. If you are a data scientist, your data persona-based learning path will be based on the fact you are a data scientist. If you are a business user, that is your persona. If you are a data analyst, your persona resides there, and so forth. There are different personas within an organization and learning should be based on those personas. The next question asked could be, "How do you create learning plans for the personas of your organization?"

That question has already been answered: through the assessments given. For some, we know their background is within the technical fields of data and analytics, and that is great, but others may not have a clue where they reside within this vast world of data. The assessments given to your organization can be varied. You may give the data scientists one assessment to find the gaps and create the learning plans, and for others, it will be a general assessment to find the comfort and skills they have with data, and everything in between. The key is to utilize the assessments to understand the organization as a whole and to find the gaps within the skills present therein.

Once those assessments are taken and individuals know their data personas, we can set in place the correct learning paths. This is the direct work of not creating one-size-fits-all approaches to data and analytical learning. Now, we understand there is something to be said for economies of scale in learning. Will you have the time to hand-craft each individual plan, especially if you are an organization of, say, 20,000 and you want all to participate over time? That would be one monumental task to unfold. Instead, work with your organization to define a set number of personas you are comfortable using. It is my experience that organizations usually land on around four personas. Then, you work to bucket those participating into those personas, put the learning paths in place for the learners, and march forward with a program.

The final question with persona-based learning can then be, "How long do these initiatives take with a persona-based learning approach?" That question also has varied answers. Now you can see why it is not a one-size-fits-all approach. Larger organizations will take longer. For example, I am currently helping an organization work on a 1.4 million-person initiative within data literacy. The reality is, you want to build a strong learning plan, know what skills you want to fit within each data persona, build proper learning for the learners, and not take too much time out of their already busy work schedules (this may mean just an hour or two of learning per week). With the overall approach becoming more customized for each organization, we are taking the necessary steps to become data driven.

Cohort approach to learning

Your Dictionary (2021) refers to a cohort as a group of people with common characteristics or support for a common cause. Think of a cohort as a group of like-minded people, a group assigned, or a group that will be going through a learning journey together. During a data literacy initiative, a cohort is a group of individuals who are going through your data literacy learning together and who are working together, meeting together, and so forth. How does a cohort learning approach go with the other points of a data literacy initiative?

First, when a group is joining a cohort, they can be assigned from your organization in many different ways. It may be that you want a whole group of data analysts to go through the initiative itself, starting with the assessment. That is a great way to approach this: taking similar positions and putting them together in a learning program from a cohort perspective. Then each individual can take the assessments given, discover their learning paths and persona, and march through your data literacy initiative with the understanding that others are in it with them and able to discuss things as a group. But the question can then come up: "What if we want to pull from different areas and not have all the same positions in the data literacy program at the same time?"

This is also an option to build your cohorts for learning. One organization I worked with had over 100,000 employees and there was no way to train everyone at once. You may say to yourself, those must have been large cohorts. On the contrary, they were quite small. For a six-month initiative, we targeted about 150 employees in total. We divided them into five cohorts of 30. Why so small if the company had 100,000 employees? Wouldn't it take forever to train all of them? Possibly, but the design of the cohorts was quite specific. Instead of just grabbing random people or people that all had "data scientist" in their title, individuals were selected to help create enthusiasm around data literacy. In turn, if done appropriately, these learners could then be a data literacy army for the organization, voicing support and desire for the whole organization to be more data literate and, in turn, more data driven.

The determination of your cohorts is up to you as an organization. Through the assessment, bucketing of the learners into the right personas, and giving the right prescriptive paths, the individuals will have opportunities to learn data and analytics, converse together, and help grow the culture to be more data driven. Note, you will want to give your cohorts opportunities to discuss together, with your data literacy leads and between themselves. Don't just give the learning paths and tell them to go "have at it." Instead, create opportunities for discussion by holding webinars, office hours, ways to create interaction among the group to discuss the program, what's working, what's not working, address questions they have about subjects, and so forth. This can be one of the powers of cohort learning, bringing people together with a common cause to become more data literate and data driven.

Metrics and measurement

Next, as we think about an initiative like data literacy, one key thing that comes up in my discussions with organizations is the ability to measure the success; organizations want to be able to see the tangible growth and acceleration of the workforce.

Two great quotes on this thought are from Peter Drucker—"if you can't measure it, you can't improve it"—and from W. Edwards Deming, which is at the beginning of the book: "In God we trust, all others must bring data" (Mackenzie, 2021).

Like other business programs, ideas, and initiatives, organizations want to be able to measure the gains they are making through a data literacy initiative. If we are going to invest our time, talent, energies, and more into a program, we want to be able to measure its success. This is something all organizations should do with a data literacy initiative and others that are closing skills gaps. We need to measure it, but how can we do so? There are multiple options.

We will not cover a comprehensive set of measurements here, that can be addressed elsewhere, but I will offer a couple of guidelines or guideposts that can help you set up your measurement. The first methodology is to use assessments and benchmarks at the start and end of your initiative. We have spoken about the assessments being used by the organization to help find the gaps in people's skills and to place them into cohort and learning persona paths, but these assessments can also be used to measure individuals' skills, backgrounds, etc., and then used as the start and end points of the initiative. By having the group retake the assessments, sizable gains and measures can be made by the learners. This can also be used to measure gains against industry benchmarks and other forms of comparative analysis with peers.

Another way to measure the gains is to have individuals take hands-on labs or assignments at the end of a program, to measure their abilities to build the right data analysis to get answers. This is a direct way to measure if certain tasks can be performed. By doing this, it can be seen if direct learning objectives were met during the data literacy program.

Overall, measurement is an absolute necessity during a data literacy initiative. Organizations need to be able to see the success that is garnered through the program. If they cannot see the measurement and growth, they could still have gaps and traps throughout the culture and skill set in an organization. As one can see, this would be a direct hindrance to a data-driven organization.

Iterative approach

One may wonder what I mean by this term "iterative approach." An iterative approach to data literacy is the understanding that things do not go perfectly. The field of statistics alone is built on probabilities. With that knowledge in mind, it should be known that as you go through a data literacy learning program at your organization, there will be bumps in the road, learnings that you must take away to make your data literacy initiative successful. Some of these bumps can be learning that different assessments aren't providing enough clarity for your organization. You may find that your organization needs more in-person training versus online. You may also find gaps in the learning where you find one course needs to be taken by each and every individual in the organization. As you go through your assessments, cohorts, persona-based learning, measurement, all of it, take the opportunity to learn from the program, improve it, put in place new initiatives, new measurements, and more. By doing all of this, your program can be truly successful and transformative for your organization.

But, don't fall into the pitfall of thinking this is a one and done thing. Data literacy is ongoing for an organization. Just think about all the new technologies and advancements happening in the world of data and analytics that will necessitate an ongoing approach to data literacy learning. Create an iterative approach that advances your culture with excitement and this can truly help you become data driven, always advancing forward.

Data literacy skills gap summary

One of my favorite quotes comes from Nelson Mandela: "I never lose. I either win or I learn" (Goodreads, 2021). This is the approach we need to take with data literacy initiatives. As we put them in place in our organizations, we need to take the opportunity to learn from failings (a lot of organizations use phrases like fail fast, etc.—well we need to truly do this) and put in place a strong culture of data and analytical learning, and data and analytical use. Doing this helps us to address the need to be truly data driven.

Remember, use the opportunity in your organization to address your data literacy skills gap. Empower your workforce to be strong with data literacy, to use data more effectively, to make data-driven decisions. Place people in cohorts, help them find their data literacy persona and skills, then help them succeed with data. Doing this can help your organization succeed with data. But, this wasn't the only skills gap that I mentioned for this chapter. There is one more: the technical data skills gap.

Data technology skills

I will not spend a lot of time on this section like I did the data literacy section. The principles shared in how to understand and run a data literacy initiative are the same for a data technology skills gap "closing" (it sounds funny to word it that way, but I think the meaning comes across). It is no secret that there is a digital and tech skills gap. We hear all the time about data literacy, digital literacy and transformation, and so forth. In the world of data and analytics, having the right tools in place is key to having the right solutions and data-driven organization. Let me turn to an example I use regularly: the work I did with a bank in Australia.

In that initiative, the bank in Australia wanted to reevaluate the tool they were using for data and analytics. Again, they did not feel they were gaining the necessary adoption of the tool. So, in turn, they blamed the tool for its lack of success. The real issue wasn't the tool, I said, but the skills gap in data literacy. But would solving data literacy just automatically gain this organization full adoption of the tool? Of course not. There has to be training on the tool, too.

When in the city of Austin, Texas, I was meeting with employees from the city of Austin itself, employees who worked for the city. I was asked a great question by an individual: What do you invest in first, the people or the technology? This is a very astute question. Most of us would say, "Of course, invest in the people first." Historically, the opposite has been done. Organizations have bought these amazing tools with the promise of data and analytical success. The reality is, it isn't an either/or scenario. If you invest first in the human skills of data literacy, then the tool will be left behind. If you invest in training on the tool alone, then the human is left behind. A marriage between the tool learning and the data literacy learning should occur.

In your case, as an organization, take the time to study what your data strategy is. With a sound understanding of your data strategy, what you are looking to accomplish, then you can figure out which tools will be needed to help your data strategy succeed. Then, you can go through and assess the organization on its data literacy and on the ability to use the tool. This combined power allows an organization to build a data-driven organization and culture because it is addressing things in the right manner. Overall, the same principles used to understand your data literacy skills gap and needs can be used to understand your organization's data technology skills and needs. Use them appropriately to build your overall initiative.

Conclusion

Far too often, organizations have bought tools and technologies with the thought that they are the strategy for the organization. Then, they have force-fit these onto the heads of the employees, hoping for usage, adoption, and stickiness to occur by magic. This is a false premise to build as your strategy. Use the time to do it right. Build your strategy, understand it. Assess your workforce, find the gaps in data skills and knowledge. Implement learning and programs to address these gaps and help the organization to be truly data driven. This is not a button you press and poof, your organization is ready. It takes time to do it right, but by doing it right, the long-term benefits can occur and you will not create tech and skills debt. You may feel it is slow, but the long-term gains can be enormous.

A personal example of this comes from my love for running trails and ultra-marathons. When I give people advice on running ultras, I tell them start slow and then go even slower, something I learned years ago. Far too often, we get excited, we go out of the gates hot, only to find we have burned ourselves out and caused our reserves to deplete. This doesn't feel like much possibly at first, but later in the race, at maybe mile 30 or 40, you may not have anything left. The same principle applies for closing data and analytical skills gaps. Don't rush out too quickly, for you may find yourself far behind later on. Instead, start intelligently, and as you move through your initiative, because of the intelligent approach you used early on, you can be more prepared to push it later on.

6

Pillars of an organizational data strategy

Strategy may be described as a planned approach to achieving a certain goal. Often, this is over a significant period of time (Merriam-Webster, 2021).

Throughout my travels and work around the world with different organizations and conferences, one large theme (and it should be distressing for the data world) emerged over and over: organizations do not have true data strategies. By a true data strategy, I mean a full, holistic strategy that ties the data, analytics, and technology being used with the data to the overall business strategy of the company. Another trend I found was that individuals did not know 1) if their company had a data strategy, or 2) what their data strategy was.

Both of these trends are not what we would call good trends and to be honest, there may have been some shift and improvement, but it is not significant or large enough to make a seismic change. Why is this? We know that organizations want to use data and to effectively be data driven, but why do we have these gaps and issues with organizational data strategy?

The purpose of this chapter is to bring to light some of the key pillars that make up an organizational data strategy. Throughout the chapter there will be principles taught that should be applied in an organization looking to be data driven. We will also examine real-life examples from my work where we can see the principles or pillars in action or where organizations have fallen short.

To begin, let us share the pillars we will be examining in our data strategy work, which all help an organization to be data driven. Those pillars are, in no set order:

- *Outcome.* What do you want to achieve and are we tying our data back to our organization's business strategy?

- *Culture.* Is our organization ready to handle being data driven (this is the most key element to being data driven)?

- *Data storage.* Are we using the right strategy to build the backend of our data philosophy and strategy?

- *Analytics.* Do we have proper use of the four levels of analytics within our organization?

- *Leadership.* Do we have the right structure and people in place to lead a data-driven strategy and do they have the right skills?

- *Tools and technology.* Do we have the right tools in place to enable our organization to succeed in a data-driven position?

- *Data literacy.* Do we have the right skill sets throughout the organization and if not, do we have the right upskilling, reskilling, and learning programs in place to ensure our data strategy is implemented properly?

- *Communication.* Do we have the proper communication in place to transmit information and data throughout the organization effectively?

- *Ethics.* Do we have the right ethical use of data in place to help us as an organization use data effectively and in the right manner?

For our purposes, we will use the rest of this chapter to cover each of these elements, the gaps and holes they can represent within an organization's ability to be data driven, but in this chapter we will not share the "how to" quite yet. We will use chapters 9–12 to help drive the "how to" throughout the different areas and pillars we will have discussed throughout the book to bring them back together to help you and your organization to be data driven.

Outcome

You may be asking yourself: what does Jordan mean by outcome? Let me tie into my personal life to describe what I mean by outcome. I have a hobby that some consider, well, they ask me, "why would you do that?" That hobby is running ultra-marathons. I love the journey, pain, etc., but there is one thing that has to be set in place before I really train, and it can be set over and over and over again: the outcome I am looking to achieve. Of course we can say to ourselves the outcome is to finish the race we are participating in, whether it is a 50-kilometer race, 50 miles, 100 miles; whatever the distance is we have signed up for, we know the outcome is to finish the race. In business, though, that is not enough. We could say with data we are looking to make better data-driven decisions. We can then turn to say, "why?" What do you mean by data driven? How will you achieve that? Is that overall or in marketing, HR, finance, etc.? As you can see, without specificity, we aren't really grasping the outcome we are looking to achieve.

Now, with that said, there are pieces we can work on to achieve something. I am, in fact, about to contradict myself in my writing. The high-level outcome you can set forth for your data strategy to ensure you are being successful with your organization's data is support for the organization's overall business strategy. That seems very intuitive, and to be fair, I think that is what a lot of people are "thinking" when they invest in data from a leadership perspective, but overall, having ideas in the air is one thing—putting them down on paper and truly knowing what to do and what to achieve is another. Yes, we should put our high-level outcome out to our organization, but that will not be enough. We must direct it, share more around it, and understand that just having an outcome will not be enough. We must fill in the gaps and work to ensure the organization can tie it back to the business.

The first thing we will discuss is that if there are many different business units and parts of an organization, how do they tie to the overall outcome? This can be a sizable gap, especially for large organizations.

Within an organization, we know, generally speaking, that we don't have one organization and one single business unit. Organizations are divided into different business units, different organizations, different areas. From this perspective, as each one of the business units and different organizations works to use data, many different gaps, holes, or issues may emerge. In this case I want to address a very common problem that spans across the globe: data silos.

Data silos

Within an organization, a very common issue in the data strategy and data-driven goals and desires is that data silos emerge. A data silo in this case is where one area, business unit, or part of the organization is walled off and using data in its own manner, process, and so forth. This issue can cause great strife within the outcome-driven approach to being data driven. As one organization works to build its own data policies, procedures, and practices, if it is not tied to a centralized outcome, the organization can suffer.

An example from my experience can be shared to illuminate that when one person or area is trying to do their own thing, that outcome-driven approach can cause more issues for an organization trying to be data driven.

During my career, I held a role where my job was to be the source of record, source of truth, for a large portion of the organization's customers. A source of record is the one source that is the truth on the data, where people should go for the data. This was during a time when the democratization of data through a business intelligence tool was a hot topic at my organization, particularly in our business unit. Remember, democratization of data is giving data to the masses. As I built out the data and information with my data engineers, one day I received a message from the assistant to the president of this group. Apparently a data point for the US consumer group had been used that did not match what I had in the system, the source of record. The individual who pulled the number had not followed procedure and went to a colleague to just pull the number for him. Without having the right definition for the data point we had built, the numbers had not matched. The result was that this number was shared publicly, and I do not know what happened to that individual who did not follow the procedure.

In the end, the reality is we see things like this happen all the time. This is one hole within the outcome-driven approach to a data-driven strategy. We need to have a centralized approach and outcome for the entire organization, then the business units can tie their data-driven work to outcomes that then flow back into the organizational outcome. That is something that needs to be understood. We are not saying every outcome will be the same across the different business units, but as the business units use data to be data driven, they can ensure that the work they do is turned to and prioritized by the over-all business outcome.

Another problem or gap that exists when not using a centralized outcome approach is that it can cause a haphazard approach to data and analytical work. What is meant in this case is when an organization is working to be data driven, without a centralized approach to outcomes, there can be different areas of the company doing different things. This type of approach can result in increased costs as different groups are buying different tools and technology; it can also cause large data issues as one group sources and stores data one way, and another sources another way.

Using an outcome-driven approach to being data driven can start an organization off on the right foot. We will touch upon how to build the right outcomes and determine them later in the book.

Culture

Have you ever tried to run some sort of strategy with a group of people, a team, an organization, that wasn't on board with what you were doing? How successful was that endeavor? Unfortunately, it probably wasn't that successful. The culture of an organization is the number one roadblock to data and analytical success. With the mind-set usually falling on data quality, data access, the tools and technology, the culture can be lost in the shuffle of the world of data, technology, and the power it impresses upon us. What does the culture mean for data and analytics?

I will define culture by the following areas for a data-driven organization: the rituals and practices, beliefs, and the skills of the organization (we have spoken on this a lot already). These key areas aren't the entirety of a data and analytics culture, of course, but I want to speak about these areas with regards to a data-driven organization.

Rituals and practices

Organizations are heaped with history and practices that have been developed over time. If each of us, especially those in leadership, thinks back on our careers or on the teams we lead now, we can find the practices, rituals, and methodologies that the teams take on. For example, in starting my career at American Express, how things were ticked and tied and checked was seen as a standard practice. Everyone should have a good grasp on these practices to make the teams work better. These rituals and practices are key to an organization utilizing data effectively. If the individuals, teams, and groups are regularly doing "business as usual" and following procedures in the manner they usually have, introducing elements of data and analytics can cause issues. Rituals and practices are key and signature to an organization succeeding.

In order for an organization to be data driven, the DNA of data needs to be woven throughout the organization. The rituals and practices need to be evolved and empowered with data and analytics. The workforce needs to feel like they are not being told that data and analytics are superseding the rituals and practices. Of course, at times data and analytics will supersede things within the organization, and we know this, change is necessary. But for an organization to succeed as a data-driven organization, data and analytics need to become lockstep with what the organization does from a ritual and practice perspective. This means that data and analytics can be tools within the rituals and practices, just like an email, video call, etc. are tools.

Beliefs

Organizations come with beliefs. Organizations come with mottos and visions. Organizations have traditions, things done on a regular basis, parties, ways to celebrate achievements. Organizations also have a personality that goes along with all that they do and a belief in what works, what doesn't work, and so forth.

If you take a step back and look at your current organization, really pondering on it and thinking through how work is done, what traditions are done on a regular basis, and how individuals think about things, you will find patterns and trends. These beliefs in how things are done are critical to success in a data-driven organization. If people do not believe data and analytics matter, if they are intimidated by the topics, or are stuck in ways and patterns that will hinder the rollout of a data-driven organization, as you can imagine it will probably fall short of any expectation or desired outcome you have.

I have an example of this in my career. While working in a data and analytical role, I wanted to upskill and in some cases probably reskill employees in how they were approaching data. The way it was being done was the traditional rollout of democratized data: I would present to them the new dashboard and data we had built as a business intelligence team, but really only focus on a typical tool training. "This is where you click and change this…" or "This is the data that is presented in this tool." This mentality had done well for us so far, but it was far below the potential of the employees in that group. Unfortunately, when I presented a new manner of training, it was shot down. The beliefs of the individuals warranted a second look, but we didn't do it. The individuals in the group were doing ok with the tools and democratized data, but it wasn't enough to truly harness the power that data and analytics can bring to an organization. Imagine if these individuals had true data literacy, knowing how to analyze and dissect data, driving insight. By building in data literacy, the beliefs in how work can be done could have been enhanced and the group become more effective.

Organizational skill sets

We have spoken at length on data literacy. The skills of the individuals in an organization matter greatly to the success of a data-driven organization AND to the culture of the organization. If people do not have the skills necessary to utilize data and analytics effectively, and feel forced to use them, you can see a revolt occur.

To improve and unleash the power of skills in an organization, among what has already been written in the book, the culture has to be one that accepts change, the evolution of skills and technology, the need to utilize change management, and the evolving of hiring practices to hire the right people in the right positions with the right skills. All of these things matter to the culture of an organization.

With regards to the skills of the organization, it isn't necessarily that everyone should be data literate instantaneously, which we know is not possible. The organization instead needs to be one of continuous learning and improvement, where challenging the status quo on skills and work is ever present, and where individuals feel not only that they can learn about data and analytics, but that it is not there to overtake their job, but to empower them. To do this, ensure your organization has a strong learning and development program. Don't just focus on "how-tos," focus on true strategic learning.

Data storage

How does your organization store its data? Is it using tried-and-true methodologies like a relational database? Is it harnessing the power of the Cloud? What is it that your organization is doing to collect and store data? The storage of data is a key element to an organization being data driven because it needs to be a key element within a data strategy. One word to note from that sentence: it is an *element* of your organization's data strategy; data storage is not a full data strategy.

How does data storage play into data strategy and a data-driven organization? First, we will not be covering specific tools and technologies or the "how to" of data storage in this book. There are plenty of resources on those areas. Instead, we want to focus on the theory behind data storage and how it fits into a holistic picture and idea around data strategy.

Data storage is just like it sounds: it is how an organization collects and stores data, making it available and powerful for end users to analyze, find insight, and communicate out with data. When an individual, business unit, or team knows what they want to utilize the data for, how they want to collect it, or even better, what question they want to answer, the storage of data and access become critical. With Cloud technology, individuals have the ability to access the data anywhere, getting insight, finding descriptive analytics or complex predictions. Overall, ease of access is a great way to drive data strategy for a data-driven organization. An example will show the power of collecting the right data and making it accessible readily and in the appropriate manner.

In a meeting with a senior leader of a food distribution company, I listened as he described how his organization was able to give powerful data and information to those working as restaurant or café managers who needed to manage employees' work hours and overtime. The data was stored and accessible in a way that these managers could easily review the necessary information on their phones. The way the organization stored data, and this was a large organization with over 200,000 employees, allowed quick access and the ability to make quick decisions. Data storage in the correct manner is powerful. Let me share an example of the reverse of this success.

While I was being recruited to one of the world's largest organizations, it was discussed with me just how messy the data and self-service analytics were for the end users. I was being brought in to build out a better infrastructure and plan with the data. This organization should already have been data driven, but alas, it was not as successful as it could have been. Like other organizations, over time multiple data sources had been built and then another, and then another. The data was a mess, without a concrete vision or plan for it. This is one of the key reasons to have a data strategy that includes data storage; by having a strategy that maps out the outcomes, desires, etc. of the data, it can be easier to build and design solutions for the data being collected. Instead, this organization was a mess, with many data sources accumulated over the years.

Analytics

In my first book, *Be Data Literate: The data literacy skills everyone needs to succeed*, I wrote extensively about the four levels of analytics, so I will not write a novel within this book on the topic, but I do want to touch upon it here in this chapter. The four levels of analytics are as follows:

Level One: Descriptive

Level Two: Diagnostic

Level Three: Predictive

Level Four: Prescriptive

A sound understanding of the four levels of analytics and how they operate within a data strategy is crucial. A colleague of mine named Donald Farmer once said that data is just an expensive cost center without analytics. Essentially, data is just data. It will just sit there unless acted upon, by human or machine, and those things need to utilize the power of the four levels of analytics for success.

While the four levels of analytics are powerful, a sound understanding is needed that an organization will not spend equal amounts of time within the different levels, in other words 25 percent in each. Also, it is necessary to know that the majority of a workforce will spend its time within levels 1 and 2: descriptive and diagnostic analytics. A small portion will be in the more technical areas of 3 and 4: predictive and prescriptive.

When we think of the four levels of analytics, a small walk-through will help to drive the point home on how the four levels work, at least in a small way:

- Within the four levels, the first is descriptive analytics. This is the "what happened" or "what is happening" level. Think about it as describing something.

- The next level, diagnostic, is where we know *why* the "what" happened in level 1. I call diagnostic analytics the *insight* level of analytics. This is power. This is where we can truly use the why behind what happened to make decisions.

- Then, in the third level we can make predictions: "We know what happened and we know why it happened. Now, if we do a, b, and c, then d, e, and f can occur."

- Finally, the fourth level is prescriptive analytics, where the data and technology can prescribe what can be done.

The four levels have power, but they must be seen as an essential part of a data strategy. In this case, there are multiple facets of how this occurs. Leaders need to hire the right talent to do the right work within the appropriate level of analytics. You aren't going to hire a data scientist who only builds data visualizations that show what happened in the past. No, you are going to want them doing data science. So, leaders need to hire and place the appropriate level of analytics on the appropriate skill set in the organization. Next, it matters what tools and technologies are used within each level of analytics. Within a data strategy, the appropriate investment in tools and technology should not only be data storage, but should include work that places the right technology into the right hands to perform the appropriate level of analytics. Hopefully you are seeing how important it is for your organization to have a holistic data strategy so corners are not cut and the organization can be data driven.

Finally, having the right skill sets to achieve the right outcome based on analytics is critical. Within data-driven organizations and strategies, we have to be able to turn the data into actionable insight. That is the end goal after all, right? To make better decisions using data? Therefore, organizations need to have the right skills in the right spots throughout the organization, so they can appropriately use the four levels of analytics for success. Please note, this also means that the leadership in an organization have the appropriate data and analytics skills in their respective roles.

Leadership

Think about your current role. If you are in a leadership position, or think of the leadership in your organization, are you or your leadership comfortable with your own data literacy skills? Does your organization have a chief data officer? Who owns the strategy of your organization? Overall, leadership of course plays a vital role within an organization's data strategy. Leadership's role has many facets that are a part of an organization's data strategy: 1) ownership, 2) investment (people and tools), 3) decision making. Of course this is not an exhaustive list, but each of these is vital to the success of a data strategy and data-driven organization. Let us examine each of these briefly.

Ownership

Leadership plays the vital role of owning the data strategy itself. This should be intuitive. Leadership owns the overall strategy and the parts of the strategy. Leadership needs to make all the decisions around data and analytics; it also needs to be accountable for the strategy and its effectiveness. Through the ownership of the strategy, leadership can work towards being data driven. As a counter, unfortunately I have seen organizations that do not have good leadership and ownership towards a data strategy. This can be catastrophic to the goal of being a data-driven organization. Have you ever tried to drive a big project without leadership's buy-in? It may fail before you really start. With leadership buy-in, you can feel the support necessary to become a data-driven organization.

Investment

Leadership owns the investment that is necessary for a data-driven organization. The investment is twofold: 1) investment in the data, tools, and technology, and 2) investment in people. Leadership must make the decisions around which tools and technologies to invest in with regards to data. This includes data storage, business intelligence tools, and other tools and technologies designed to help organizations succeed with data. Investment also means investing in people. By this we are not just talking about the hiring of people, but the investment in upskilling and reskilling.

It should be noted: leadership needs to ensure proper investment is a combination of both people and the tools and technology. Investing in one or the other, without line of sight and proper packaging together, can cause issues. Ensure your organization is investing in both.

Decision making

Finally, leadership is where the final straw lands. When it comes to the overall decision making through the organization on data, it is owned by leadership and it can be delegated, of course. Leadership should empower the organization to be data driven by democratizing data-driven decision making throughout. But, the accountability is owned by leadership. Decision making is the essence of data and analytical work. Leadership needs to be data literate, strong in its communication skills, and then drive strong decisions through the organization using data.

Tools and technology

We have spoken about tools and technology in the book already, but a quick synopsis of where they fall in a data strategy is important. I want to speak of tools and technology maybe a bit differently than you would think. Usually, one would describe which tools and technologies fall under what data and application of data. In this case, I want to speak of one thing not to do with tools and technology with regards to data, and how they should fall within your data strategy.

One thing I like to make abundantly clear is that a tool or technology is not a strategy. That is it. Final line. A tool or technology is an enabler of a data strategy. Now, you may be saying to yourself that you know this, but unfortunately, historically speaking, this is how organizations have operated around the world for years. They invest in a new tool within data, say a business intelligence tool, and then "force" that upon their workforce and say this is what you will be using. The tool became the strategy. There are many potential flaws that can occur this way, such as the tool not truly working for the needs of the workforce to build a data-driven organization.

Another potential flaw that arises from a love of tools and technology is one I have also seen: a love of the outcome of the tool and technology. The prime example of this occurring is how organizations and individuals fall in love with data visualization and that is where they place their trust and investment. Data visualizations are powerful and important parts of an organization's data strategy, but they are just a part of it. This tool and technology outcome became the face of data and analytics for the vast number of end users, but it is just a piece of the four levels of analytics. By falling in love with the outcome, the organization can be stuck in descriptive analytics.

Tools and technology are powerful enablers for a data strategy to work, but that is what they are. Tools and technologies should be assessed by and through the organization's data strategy. When an organization knows the skill set of the workforce, has an understanding of the outcomes to be achieved, etc., then it can find the right tool that will enable that to occur. It is like going to the gym and finding the right weights for you to use to accomplish your workout. When you are trying to accomplish a task, an outcome, the right tools can facilitate and help you achieve the outcome.

Data literacy

The book has covered the topic of data literacy in depth, but here I want to speak of its place within a data strategy. Like tools and technology, data literacy is an enabler of the data strategy your organization will put in place. Imagine your organization has the things in place for a data strategy: leadership is well skilled, you have invested in the right tools and technology, you are using the Cloud effectively, but yet, your data and analytical work adoption is low. You aren't seeing a return on the investment you have made.

For an organization to realize true data and analytical potential, part of the strategy must be the reskilling, upskilling, and continuous learning that is data literacy. By having this as part of an organization's workflow, you can see better adoption of the data strategy you have put in place. My work with the financial services firm speaks here. When they walked me through their data literacy strategy, it was the inverse of what we are discussing. They had built a data literacy strategy, but didn't know the organization's data strategy. In this case, how could they know what to teach if they didn't know what that organization was looking to do with data? We must know what an organization wants to do with data, and then the data literacy learning can be put in place.

Communication

You may ask yourself why I am listing communication as a part of your organization's data strategy. Let me ask you the question again: How many of you like to get an email that says you have mandatory training to do? When I ask that question in person, I hear the chuckle of laughter from people who know what I am referring to. People don't like getting notices or emails that mandate something to occur. In this case, if an organization does not have a proper communication strategy in place to help it adopt the data strategy effectively, then it may fall flat.

In our case, a communication plan is really focused on helping the workforce to know "why" the data strategy is such. Focus first on a communication around the "why" of the data strategy. You can then go into the "what" and the "how." With the right communication strategy in the data strategy, these things go together in their holistic approach. This can enable you to roll out the program with a more effective change management approach.

Another communication resource I recommend organizations use is thought leadership webinars to kick off or excite the workforce to what is coming through a data strategy. Using webinars that discuss the why, what, and how can paint a picture at the beginning of what is to come, how the organization will do this, why the organization is approaching it in such a way, and more. If your organization is already doing data work and it feels like you don't know how to go back, you can. Take the time to find ways to communicate more effectively and regularly. Find ways to bring the thought leadership in to allow individuals to internalize what is happening, how they are a part of it (this can be a huge catalyst for success, helping individuals know their part), and to really establish a "why" for the organization.

Ethics

This may seem like an odd section to have within data strategy, but it is very real. I am sitting and writing this in the year 2021 and over the past few years, the ethical use of data has become a hot topic. From black box algorithms to biased results, the world of data is undergoing scrutiny that it hasn't before. As technologies and data advance at incredible rates, as data becomes more and more entrenched within organizational work, and as artificial intelligence and machine learning become more prevalent in the world, these tools, technologies, and data need to be used in an ethical manner.

In a 2020 article for McKinsey, Janiszewska-Kiewra et al argue that having and enforcing a good policy for ethical uses of data can be a competitive advantage. Customers are increasingly concerned for their data privacy and therefore may prioritize providers that offer full transparency. Unless ethics is a priority on the CEO's agenda, negligence can result in reputational consequences or even the shutdown of the business. Companies need formal programs for standards to ensure they are upheld and evaluated regularly.

I love how it says that it is a competitive advantage for businesses to have a good policy in place on the ethical use of data. Why? First, consumers like transparency. We live in a day and age where transparency can be key. Second, we live in an era where people want to see the right thing done. By having a good policy on data ethics in place at your company, you can then show the world and consumers how you use it effectively. Finally, not having a policy could bring damage to your company if you use data inappropriately and it becomes public knowledge. This could cause fines or other issues. Ensure you have a policy that covers ethical use of data.

Overall, as part of your data strategy and to be truly data driven, ensure your organization has a policy in place around the ethical use of data.

Conclusion

The importance of having a solid data strategy in place cannot be overstated. We are living in a time when so much power and technology is at our fingertips. Data is flowing all around us and organizations have the opportunity to be truly data driven. To be truly data driven requires the right strategy in place. Remember the key pillars of this strategy:

- *Outcome.* What do you want to achieve and are we tying our data back to our organization's business strategy?

- *Culture.* Is our organization ready to handle being data driven (this is the most key element of being data driven)?

- *Data storage.* Are we using the right strategy to build the backend of our data philosophy and strategy?

- *Analytics.* Do we have a proper use of the four levels of analytics within our organization?

- *Leadership.* Do we have the right structure and people in place to lead a data-driven strategy and do they have the right skills?

- *Tools and technology.* Do we have the right tools in place to enable our organization to succeed in a data-driven position?

- *Data literacy.* Do we have the right skill sets throughout the organization and if not, do we have the right upskilling, reskilling, and learning programs in place to ensure our data strategy is implemented properly?

- *Communication.* Do we have the proper communication in place to transmit information and data throughout the organization effectively?

- *Ethics.* Do we have the right ethical use of data in place to help us as an organization to use data effectively and in the right manner?

The right strategy, owned by leadership, can help an organization thrive. Let me end this chapter with two powerful quotes on data strategy:

> Today, the value of data is well understood. Rather than seeing data as a byproduct of various business activities, most organizations understand it's a valuable resource. Unlocking that value, however, can be a

challenge. Organizations might not know how to answer the question, "What is big data?" They also might not understand what data to collect or how to effectively capture it. Once they collect data, they also face the challenge of converting it into a useful form, sharing it across the organization and deriving insights from it. A data strategy gives employees guidance on how to do these things and helps ensure people across the organization do so in a consistent manner. (Lotame, 2019)

I love the word "insights." In the end, the goal of a data strategy should be the empowerment of the organization to use data to find insights and to lead them to decisions.

Finally, from my colleague Bernard Marr:

Having a clear data strategy is absolutely vital when you consider the sheer volume of data that is available these days. I see too many businesses get so caught up in the Big Data buzz that they collect as much data as possible, without really considering what they want to do with all that data. While others are so overwhelmed by options that they bury their head in the sand. Neither represent a smart way to run a business.

Instead of starting with the data itself, every business should start with strategy. At this stage, it doesn't matter what data is out there, what data you're already collecting, what data your competitors are collecting, or what new forms of data are becoming available. Neither does it matter whether your business has mountains of analysis-ready data at your disposal, or next to none. A good data strategy is not about what data is readily or potentially available—it's about what your business wants to achieve, and how data can help you get there. (Marr, 2021)

Learn your organization's data strategy. If your organization doesn't have one, be the one to start it.

7

The gap in leadership

Merriam-Webster refers to leadership as an ability to lead others (2021). How many of you would feel comfortable leading your business unit, team, organization, or others within your business in the world of data and analytics? Do you have a good, solid grip on the four levels of analytics? Are you comfortable with your data literacy skills and ability to make sound, smart decisions with data? Do you feel you could help build and execute a data strategy? All of these skills should be positioned within leadership in an organization; they are critical to being a data-driven organization.

In this chapter we will look at two levels of leadership within an organization: the executive leadership team and then the team leaders and decision makers throughout the organization. If the executive team is the one that puts in place the strategy, the team leadership, managers, and decision makers are tasked with the execution of that strategy. We will talk about the gaps and skills within each of these areas to ensure they are executed properly and done well in the organization. On the executive side, we will talk about the skills needed to lead an organization from a data strategy on down, helping the organization to be data driven (hint: if you do not have a chief data officer in your organization, get ready to hear you need one). On the second level of leadership, we will talk about the skills gap in regard to the skills needed to help the executive and lead out on a data-driven strategy.

Executive leadership

In the world of data and analytics, leadership principles hold true for organizations looking to be data driven. There are skills needed to drive forward with success in data and analytics, and unfortunately, they are not fully being met. Leadership knows the need for data and analytics, but you can't just throw money at it and expect success. There need to be strong leadership skills that allow the organization to succeed now and into the future. That is one of the keys of leadership in data and analytics that is an absolute necessity: leadership that can evolve, advance, and adapt to the changing world of data and analytics.

The thought above that leadership needs new skills within data and analytics, really skills that adapt to the future, comes to us from the Center for Creative Leadership: "Simply put, the leadership gap is how aligned current leadership is with what's thought to be important for leadership effectiveness in the future."

Current research shows that leaders aren't adequately prepared for the future. This finding is consistent across countries, organizations, and levels in the organization (Center for Creative Leadership, 2020). In leadership, there are many older principles that are adopted and adapted: "this is the way we have always done it" or "this is the principle I learned." Unfortunately, this type of attitude towards leadership is a "stuck" attitude. The world of data and analytics, and really the world of technology, is advancing, evolving. For example, I know of a business that is looking into the food service industry. The company is not a food service company, but a data company. That is the value. It had been met with some resistance based on this new way of doing things in its specific niche. This mentality can be detrimental to leadership and a data-driven organization.

For executive leadership, we want to cover the following areas:

- *Data literacy*. Executive leaders must have data literacy confidence, with a mindset for continuous learning.
- *Digital literacy*. Executive leaders must have a sound understanding of technology and its empowerment (think the Cloud).

- *Change management.* Leadership needs to have a sound understanding of change management principles to adapt and evolve with data and analytics (Center for Creative Leadership, 2020).

- *Strategic thinking.* Do leaders truly know how to strategically think through data and analytical strategies? What they want to do with data (Neal, 2021)?

- *Chief data officer.* Does your organization have the right leadership in place for data and analytical success?

- *Communication.* One key with data and analytics is transparent, effective communication.

Overall, you can see through studies and articles that the leadership skills of the future are those that are adaptive, evolving, digitally and data literate, and with strong communication and strategy skills. Let's cover each of these topics as a part of leadership, with its goal to be data driven. Remember, data is there to help enhance and empower an organization to make better decisions. Each of the pillars for executive leadership is essential for a data-driven organization, and we will touch upon each within the skill sets and abilities of leaders.

Data literacy

We have spoken at length about data literacy, but data literacy is a continuous learning process. Remember the definition of data literacy: the ability to read, work with, analyze, and communicate with data. In the 2021 study by Qlik, it was found that only 32 percent of the C-suite was data literate (Qlik, 2021). If that is the number driving a data-driven organization, we are experiencing a large skills gap in data literacy within executive leadership. Why does data literacy matter so much for executive leadership?

We have covered this in depth in this book, but data literacy is key to success with data and analytics, especially when it comes to the leadership of the organization. First, the senior leaders of the company, the executives, need to set the tone. That is one of the most important parts to cover here; the leaders of the organization need to set the example for all the other employees in the company. By proving that it takes its example seriously, the C-suite shows the organization it means business.

Along with the example, an executive team that understands data literacy and its importance will work towards continuous learning. This is a must. If you read at the beginning of this chapter the different skills that leadership must have for data-driven success, the ability to evolve, adapt, and understand the future and its trends is a part of data literacy. With data literacy, the executive leadership team will understand the importance of data ethics, the Cloud, data engineering, data science, data governance, data visualizations, machine learning and artificial intelligence, and whatever other areas of data and analytics you want to discuss. This strong, data-literate executive team will be empowered and enabled to deal with the current data situation within the organization, and able to adapt for the future. Strong data literacy eliminates one aspect of the skills gap by putting the team in a position to succeed.

For data literacy to succeed, leadership needs to understand that it is not something you accomplish and arrive at, like passing an exam. Data literacy is ongoing and needs to be understood as such. Along with this, leadership must not rest on its laurels and feel they know it or are good with it. This is the opposite of the mindset needed for data-driven success.

Digital literacy

The book has spoken of data literacy in multiple areas, but why are we now bringing in the close friend, twin, sibling, whatever you want to call it, of digital literacy? The American Library Association (ALA) defines digital literacy as "The ability to use information and communication technologies to find, evaluate, create, and communicate information, requiring both cognitive and technical skills" (Renaissance, 2021). Digital literacy involves a key and powerful aspect of data literacy and being data driven: the understanding of the right technologies used to solidify the work of a data-driven organization.

In a data-driven organization, the tools and technologies used for data and those not data specific must interact and be a part of the entirety of the organization. As an organization invests in communication tools, like Slack or Microsoft Teams, as individuals work to communicate effectively with data, like in data literacy, they will need access to these tools and the skills to use them. Executives need to not only know the data and analytic tools, but also how these tools will interact together with the rest of the organization's tools. Here, the work of a chief information officer or chief technology officer is crucial. This work needs to be combined with the work of the senior leader in data, hopefully a chief data officer (which we will speak of later in this chapter). By having digital literacy in the executive suite, you can find more success with your data-driven organization.

Change management

In a book on being data driven, why would we have a portion that dives into the world of change management? Isn't that the work of big consulting firms, human resources, or other areas? Why does leadership need to be a part of the program? Change management might be the secret sauce you need to succeed in being a data-driven organization. Let's dive in to find out why.

To help us set the tone for understanding why change management matters, let me pull in how I will be defining change management: "The application of a structured process and set of tools for leading the people side of change to achieve a desired outcome" (Prosci, 2021). Basically, change management is how an organization deals with change, making it successful. That definition right there should show all leaders reading this book why they need to really understand change management principles, not just turn it over to others to lead.

Going back to Qlik's study:

- 24 percent of business decision makers are fully confident in their data literacy abilities;
- 78 percent of business decision makers said they would be willing to invest more time and energy into improving their data skill sets;

- 94 percent of respondents using data in their current role agree that data helps them do their jobs better and they also believe greater data literacy would give them more credibility (82 percent) in the workplace;

- 21 percent of 16- to 24-year-olds are data literate, suggesting schools and universities are failing to ensure students have the skills they need to enter the working world (The Data Literacy Project, 2021a).

This last metric can shock people, who may say, "Isn't that generation already data literate?" No. The answer is they are technology literate, but they don't necessarily know how to use data. Now, looking over just those four metrics, let me show you a couple more from a different Qlik study:

- 32 percent of business executives surveyed said that they're able to create measurable value from data.

- 27 percent of business executives said their data and analytics projects produce actionable insights (The Data Literacy Project, 2021b).

The final metrics come from a study commissioned by Qlik that shows us what value will come from stronger data literacy, and therefore a better data-driven organization:

- Organizations with strong data literacy, enterprises that had data literacy scores in the study were valued at $320–$534 million higher in enterprise value (The Data Literacy Project, 2021c).

To improve data and digital literacy throughout an organization, to enable and empower leadership to grow with continuous learning, to think strategically and then roll things out through an organization, change management principles are necessary. The interconnectedness of organizations and teams, whether on location or virtual/remote, necessitates change management principles for leadership.

Through change management, there are many principles and rules leadership can follow to empower the organization's data-driven success. Throughout this book, I want to focus on just two: involve every layer, and assess and adapt (Aguirre and Alpern, 2014).

First, involving every layer is necessary within a data-driven organization. The days of having just one team doing all the work or being involved with data and analytics are far gone. When leadership learns and adopts change management principles to help the organization succeed with data, they must consider all areas of the organization. No hand-offs. No easy ways out. Change management must involve every layer, but like other things, it is not a one size fits all. Find what change management needs to be done in different areas of the organization. This can empower the organization's success.

The second principle I want to focus on for change management, which is a theme within data and analytics, is assess and adapt. Data and analytics is a field of learning, of growth, of evolving, adapting, redoing models and analyses, etc. The change management principles you develop and envelop in the organization must be those that are adaptable. You will learn, you will grow, you will find new areas to improve the change management program within data and analytics. Allow this to happen and set your organization up for success.

Strategic thinking

This is an area of executive leadership I think most organizations feel like they deploy and is a part of what they do already. This may be true, but it is becoming an even bigger imperative in the world of data-driven organizations and advancements in technology. There are many ways to look at strategic thinking, but we need to think of it as a way to feel for the future, especially as the future is uncertain, ever changing, and becoming more and more driven by data, AI, and machine learning. As technology advances, so must leadership. There must be strategic foresight for the future, to adapt, evolve, and succeed.

Effective Governance gives the following definitions of strategic thinking:

- Strategic thinking focuses on finding and developing unique opportunities to create value by enabling a provocative and creative dialogue among people who can affect an organization's direction, i.e. the board and management.

- It is the input to strategic planning. Good strategic thinking uncovers potential opportunities for creating value and challenges assumptions about an organization's value proposition, so that when the strategic plan is created, it targets these opportunities.

- Strategic thinking is a way of understanding the fundamental drivers of a business and challenging conventional thinking about them, in discussion with others.

- Finally, strategic thinking is having an awareness of what has not yet taken shape, having foresight (Effective Governance, 2021).

There are many aspects of the list above that are necessary for leadership to be data driven and help the organization use data for its empowerment. First, we read that strategic thinking enables "a provocative and creative dialogue among people who can affect" the direction of the organization. As the world continues to adapt and evolve from the growth in data and technology over the past decade, plus the advent of Covid-19 and the futuristic advancements coming, the ability to have creative and challenging dialogue around data and analytics will be necessary. Here we see that need for a sound understanding of data and analytics again, but also the ability to think beyond what is in front of us. If you find yourself not feeling comfortable with this way of thinking, meaning the ability to think abstractly and creatively about the future, the need to empower your organization further in these areas, and to be able to walk the walk, take the time to learn how and feel comfortable in this space. To do this, you can find books on critical thinking, adapting to change, etc. Like most topics in data and analytics, studying and then putting it into practice can help.

Second, in the quote above, we read that strategic thinking should also be about unlocking potential opportunities for the organization and challenging assumptions about the value proposition and plans of the organization. I want you to think back to where you were in

January 2020. Were you thinking that in about two months' time, your life would be altered drastically, meaning permanently? Were you thinking that economies around the world would shut down, employees would largely be working remotely, and that the power of data would become even more necessary? I am guessing the answer to these questions for most people is "no," but that is what happened. Assumptions were challenged for individuals and organizations around the world. Executives needed to be able to adapt, quickly. My calendar blew up as organizations were not ready to use data to make decisions when it was needed most. That ability to think strategically to survive, adapt, and be the most effective during a challenging time was necessary. Now, don't get me wrong, organizations did well during the pandemic. They worked things out during unprecedented times. The ability to think strategically around data and analytics could have helped them to be even more successful.

Third, the quote states that strategic thinking is about challenging the fundamental drivers of a business. As executives use their data literacy skills to make decisions about data, and look to the future to understand potential shifts, changes, and evolutions to the business, economies, and world as a whole, the organization can change the fundamental course of the business. This was a necessity through the pandemic and will continue to be so as the future evolves more and more. As we see the advent and growth of artificial intelligence and machine learning, we will see the need for organizations to adapt more and more. Executives must challenge the fundamental drivers of the business. As I mentioned earlier regarding the food service business, it wasn't food service, it was data that was the business driver.

Finally, strategic thinking is having an awareness of what has not taken shape, having foresight. I feel we have covered this, but it needs to be stated clearly: we do not know what the future holds. The world is moving faster, becoming more global, and we need executives who can make smart decisions about the future of data. There are examples of businesses that had opportunities to participate in the future economies of the world, to succeed, but instead they held onto older norms or ways of doing things, whatever they were. Unfortunately, some of these businesses are no longer around, or if they are, are not what they were in the past. Had they had strategic thinking in place, being truly data driven, they may have survived.

Overall, develop strong strategic thinking within your executive leadership team.

Chief data officer

From an executive leadership perspective, this section of this chapter may be the most important. The role of chief data officer (CDO) needs to be on the minds of every organization, whether the role is active in the organization or not. The first-appointed CDO role was at Capital One in 2002, and by 2018 around 67.9 percent of businesses surveyed reported having a CDO (Forbes Insights, 2019).

What is a chief data officer exactly, or, what should a chief data officer be? Let's just say there is some confusion on what the role is, who owns what, etc. From the same article discussing how many organizations had CDOs in 2018, we read that, based on recent executive surveys by NewVantage, there was little clarity on a CDO's primary responsibilities. Thirty-nine percent said it was setting data strategy in their organization, while 60 percent believed that that responsibility was held by C-suite executives or that no one role was accountable for data.

This is an interesting insight into the world of a CDO and why it becomes so vastly important for the executive team to understand, utilize, and empower the organization to use data correctly.

One key reason for this ambiguity about the role of the CDO is that a delineation of responsibilities is not clear or has not been set forth, according to the *Forbes* article, especially with regards to the difference in responsibilities between the chief information officer (CIO) and the CDO. Historically, the CIO may have owned some of the responsibilities that are now seen as those of the CDO. This lack of understanding of who owns what, where, and why can cause confusion and lead the organization to have disjointed data work.

Overall, this section of the chapter is going to set forth the ideas and needs of the CDO. Those include the following:

- data strategy
- data governance
- data center of excellence, with a hybrid approach (I will explain this more)
- data literacy (Morrell, 2021)
- innovation (Olavsrud and Zetlin, 2020)
- analytics (Olavsrud and Zetlin, 2020)

These key responsibilities help to shift, change, and evolve an organization to be data driven. Note that while the CDO owns these responsibilities, it is up to the whole organization to help run these data perspectives and needs succinctly and properly. Let's examine each.

DATA STRATEGY

We have spoken much about data strategy and we will speak even more about it in a later chapter when we discuss how to build your data strategy. For the perspective of this chapter, we want to discuss that the onus and ownership of the data strategy should fall on the shoulders of the CDO, with the rest of the executive team and organization helping to bring it to fruition.

In conjunction with the rest of the executive team, the CDO should have strong business acumen. The CDO will work with the different areas of the business, particularly the leadership of the different departments (think the chief marketing officer, chief financial officer), to understand what that business line is doing, what its data needs to look like, and how the CDO and data strategy can help that line of business. Through this work, the CDO will need to have strong business acumen to understand what the business is trying to do, what each business unit looks to accomplish, and to ensure the data strategy is falling in line with the business strategy.

This last part is one of the key responsibilities of the CDO: ensure that the data work and strategy is helping empower and enable the organization's business strategy. The CDO must ensure the organization is not getting caught up in fads and other hype and buzz, allowing silos and other data errors to occur. The CDO is that centralized role that allows the sync and flow between the business strategy and the data strategy.

DATA GOVERNANCE

According to Stedman and Vaughan (2020), data governance is a process of managing the data in enterprise systems based on internally driven standards and policies. This process incorporates the availability, usability, integrity, and security of the data. Therefore, effective data governance ensures data consistency and trustworthiness, and puts standards in place to prevent misuse. New privacy regulations and the increased use of data analytics mean that data governance is imperative for organizations.

Data governance is a critical role for the CDO and should be worked on together with the CIO. With the evolution of data, technology, and their use, data governance has become more critical (especially during the pandemic, where misuse and misunderstanding of data became more widespread, with repercussions still occurring. Note, this came from all areas, political spectrums, etc.). The data strategy should include a portion on data governance. As the definition above sets forth, as data is being utilized more for decision making and to optimize operations, internal processes, etc., the governance and accessibility of data are of utmost importance. As we continue to produce more and more data, and as organizations look to use, sell, and profit from data, the governance of your organization's data is key.

DATA CENTER OF EXCELLENCE (HYBRID APPROACH)

This may be something that you don't think of regularly but should be a part of your organization's data strategy, and should be owned by the CDO. The approach organizations take to using and operating in data can take multiple forms. One form you can see is a pure data center of excellence, through which all data and analytics operate and then are filtered out through the organization. This approach can be effective as the teams know who to go through and who owns the data work; the data strategy is owned and run through the center of excellence. This approach can also help with the democratization of data as it allows the organization to have the central team own the work, but then for the end users of the data to analyze the results. The downside of a true center of excellence approach is that the data is all owned and managed by that center of excellence.

The second approach to data work is to not have a center of excellence, but for each business unit to own its own data and have it spread out. This can be good because the business unit will have a direct tie into the data strategy, but because of the spread-out approach, some organizations may feel that ownership or even a CDO is unnecessary. This spread-out approach can cause issues because although the organization has an overall data strategy, each unit is doing its own thing, thereby potentially causing issues. Without the role of CDO in place or with everything spread so thin, the organization may find the work of data is not as strong as it should be.

I advise a hybrid approach. This is where you have a center of excellence within data, led by the organization's CDO, but then each business unit also runs data and analytics. With each business unit running data and analytics, it all rolls up through the organization's hybrid center of excellence. Through this centralized approach with the center of excellence, plus each business unit having its own data teams (that report or get direction from the CDO center of excellence), organizations can have the best of both worlds, plus the control and governance necessary for the organization to succeed with data.

DATA LITERACY

One paragraph will suffice here. The CDO must own your organization's data literacy programs. First off, your CDO must be data literate. That may seem funny, but in some organizations you can bet people are promoted to the CDO position when they have no business being in that role. Second, the CDO needs to make learning an imperative throughout the organization. We have said it enough in this book, but the world is consistently changing in its use of data. The CDO must establish a culture of continuous learning. They must set the example. Having strong data literacy upskilling and reskilling means having programs in place that are continuous, where individuals can test their skills, try out new things, and utilize the tools and technologies effectively in order to succeed in their jobs and with data.

INNOVATION

As was mentioned above, the world is evolving and shifting rapidly. The CDO must be prepared for this world that we do not yet know, plus be ready to shift and evolve. Another aspect of innovation for the CDO is their ability to be creative. The world of data and analytics has been seen at times as 1) boring, and 2) intimidating. With the majority of a workforce not data literate or confident with data, by eliminating the intimidation portion of data and analytics, the CDO can help the workforce to succeed. The "boring" aspect can be improved with data literacy.

Overall, though, the CDO needs to be creative in the utilization of data and analytics throughout the organization. They need to try new methodologies, try new things. One key thing the CDO can do for innovation is to get a diverse set of voices to the table to discuss projects. Don't just get a team of statisticians and data scientists together to solve a problem. The CDO can bring those with an arts background to the table. Get those who usually don't have, or feel they have, a voice. Allow the creativity and experience of different people to come and drive the innovation of analytics, data methodologies, data visualizations, and data storytelling to the organization. Your organization has many creative and powerful voices that can help in data and analytics. It is up to you and the CDO to allow them a seat at the table.

ANALYTICS

The role of CDO is no longer just in charge of managing the data of the company. This may have historically been the top mandate, but it goes beyond that now. Your organization's CDO needs to also lead the charge with analytical work. This means the four levels of analytics, understanding and staffing the workforce appropriately, ensuring the hybrid center of excellence, are all centered around strong analytics. This also means they drive and work through the holistic data strategy in the company, which then leads to the true and correct approach to the business strategy support data should be. Unfortunately, too many organizations focus squarely on the data side of the strategy, although this is important (far too many companies have messy data). Combine that side of the strategy with the correct work of analytics, and the right approach to data and analytics can be built together.

CHIEF DATA OFFICER CONCLUSION

If your organization does not have a CDO, get one. If you do have one, ensure that they are focusing their work in the right manner and right areas. Having this position is not a nice to have. It is essential. Having it work properly is even more important. Just because an organization has a CDO, it doesn't mean it has arrived. Every organization should evaluate its work to ensure it is being done properly.

Communication

One of the biggest gripes I have heard throughout my career, in any aspect of business, is about transparent communication. I think a lot of organizations use catchy phrases like "we will be transparent" quite often, but they aren't. I can remember a point in my career, during a critical time, being told the company would be transparent and we didn't really hear anything for two to three months. Within data and analytics, communication is key.

Within data and analytics communication, stick to the motion of starting with why, then progressing to the what, and ending with the how. Teach the organization why data and analytics matters, why you are driving a data-driven organization and initiatives within data literacy. Establishing why you are doing something is key to getting people on board. Please, please, please do not send "You have mandatory training" emails. This is a quick way to not get adoption. Instead, start with communications around the importance of data, why your organization is taking it on, etc. Use thought leadership and webinars to help drive this forward.

Once you have established your why, then proceed to describe what. Describe what a data-driven organization is. Describe and define data literacy for your organization. Lay out the strategy and plans in a "what" manner: what it is, which teams will do what, etc. Then you can lay out the groundwork with how: how you are going to do it, how you will build teams, how you will upskill and reskill.

Establish proper communication throughout the organization. To do this, ensure you establish better data fluency, the language of data spoken throughout the organization. We will speak on this portion more when we go through the next chapter on culture.

Executive leadership: summary

Before we go into the next section of this chapter, which is the next tiers of leadership, let's summarize the executive leadership side. Remember the key areas of executive leadership:

- data literacy
- digital literacy
- change management (Center for Creative Leadership, 2020)
- strategic thinking (Neal, 2021)
- chief data officer
- communication

With a strong understanding of these areas, you can establish and fill in the skills gaps that exist within your executive leadership team.

Tiered leadership

I call this next group of leadership within data and analytics "tiered leadership." This level of leadership is not like the executive leadership, as that is one level. This is all leadership that reports up through the executives of the organization, through different lineages. So, this could be the manager level, just starting up in leadership, on through to the senior vice president level or general managers, presidents, and all shapes and sizes in between. These levels need to develop areas of leadership just like the executives, with data literacy, communication, and the list presented above. In this section, we need to describe the main difference in this level: the execution of the data strategy through the teams these leaders manage. This right here is the key to this level of leadership. The executives will establish the vision and strategy; the next tiers of leadership are responsible for the execution. How do they do this?

First, this level of leadership needs to have a sound understanding of the data strategy. You may be saying to yourself if you find yourself in this position, "but I do have a good understanding." I can appreciate the confidence, but I need this level of leadership to be really good at clarifying questions and answers for the strategy. Data is a different type of strategy. At this level of leadership not only do you need to understand what the strategy is, but you need to understand clearly your role and level within that strategy. Obviously, if you are a leader within the data and analytics space, you are building models, visualizations, or doing other things within data and analytics. Your understanding is different than that of, say, a director of marketing. The director of marketing is not responsible for the advanced and technical sides of data and analytics, but they are responsible for the end users, the interpretation of data, etc.

Second, this level of leadership needs to allow the open and honest use of data. What I mean by this is that leadership needs to allow time for individuals to use and get better with data. Let's face it, individuals have busy jobs. Data should not supersede this. With data literacy initiatives to help establish a data-driven organization, we don't want individuals to feel that it is taking over their roles and responsibilities. Instead, make openings, time, and places for individuals to learn. Sometimes this means an honest evaluation from leaders to find what truly needs to be done and what doesn't. Run an audit of your team's work to help understand what can and can't be removed. Being data driven doesn't mean we need everyone using data at every minute of the day, but it does mean leadership is in the position to help the organization succeed correctly with data.

Third, ensure your own comfort and confidence with data if you are a leader, first and foremost. If you are not a leader, do the same. Then, ensure that of your teams. Again, we are talking about the key piece of data literacy, but it really is that important.

With the understanding of the tiered leadership, how do we ensure they know how to do this correctly? How do we ensure they know how to roll this out appropriately? We go back to training, communication, a sound strategy, and that term and business practice of change management. There are plenty of books for those fields, including programs for the improvement of data literacy and data programs, so we will not get exhaustive in this book. Study, reach out, and find those programs and leaders who know how to drive and help leadership lead a data-driven approach.

Conclusion

Overall, as can be seen in this chapter, it is necessary for leadership to truly understand data and analytics, have a sound strategy in place for success, and an overall approach for being data driven. For data-driven success, we truly need to have a leadership suite from the executives to the tiered leadership levels who have a sound understanding of these principles. For organizations to be data driven, leadership must fill in its gaps. By doing so, the organization can see better data and analytical adoption, and truly enjoy the fruits of its data investments.

8

The biggest hurdle: culture

We have spoken already in this book on culture, but this chapter is going to focus on the key data-driven culture characteristics that organizations need to have in place to ensure success. Remember, we spoke of the rituals, beliefs, etc. of the organization. In order for an organizational culture to be in place, there are a few characteristics each organization needs to ensure are a part of it. The following characteristics will be described throughout this chapter:

- *Data fluency.* Does your organization speak the language of data?
- *Adaptability.* Are your employees well armed and trained to deal with change, including the shift and evolution of their roles?
- *Continuous learning.* We know about learning, but are your employees in a sound position to succeed with continuous learning?
- *Diversified skill sets.* Are you hiring employees with diverse backgrounds or are you only looking for the same advanced, technical skills like data science?
- *Growth vs fixed mindset.* Are they armed with a growth mindset?
- *Gamification and rewards-based systems.* Do you have a good rewards-based system in place to reward your employees' work within your data-driven organization?
- *Embracing failure.* You may say the adage "fail fast," but do you truly adopt it?

- *Clear vision and strategy.* Do your employees know and embrace your data strategy?
- *Grassroots.* Does your organization employ both a top-down AND a bottom-up approach?
- *Recognition of biases.* Does your organization recognize and understand its biases within?

These are key characteristics of a data-driven culture. As I state over and over, the number one roadblock to your data and analytical success, to being data driven, will be your culture. Understanding change management, which was brought up in the last chapter, and knowing how to influence your organization's culture to utilize data will empower you to be data driven. Each of these principles has a purpose.

Data fluency

Data fluency, sometimes intermingled or interchanged with data literacy, is the ability to speak a common language of data throughout an organization. Can you speak with fluency in data? Can you walk the walk and talk the talk?

> Like being fluent in a language, data fluency enables people to express ideas about data in a shared language. In a business context, data fluency connects employees across roles through a set of standards, processes, tools and terms. Data-fluent employees can turn piles of raw data into actionable information because they understand how to interpret it, know the data that is and isn't available, as well as how to use it appropriately. Data fluency rejects the idea that only a select few are gatekeepers of information, instead spreading knowledge, widening data access across an organization, and as a result, improving decision-making for everyone. (ThoughtSpot, 2021)

This ability to converse and speak the language of data throughout an organization is of pivotal importance; it empowers the connectivity of data throughout the business. Data fluency opens up many doors through the organization for the data strategy to be successful. How can an organization develop more data fluency?

First, develop a common data dictionary. A data dictionary is just like it sounds, a dictionary for data terminology, etc. Without a data dictionary, an organization can run with different parts of the business defining things differently without knowing it. Now, terms can be defined differently depending on context, but that is on purpose. If done unknowingly, the organization can run into issues like my career saw when I was the source of record and someone pulled a number from a colleague. When this did not match my numbers, it caused confusion. I also had a conversation where an executive mentioned the headcount of an organization that was different than the official HR headcount, but both were actually accurate, depending on how it was reported, defined, or sourced. A common data dictionary defines, empowers, and enables individuals to work with data more effectively.

Second, build your data literacy by creating a strategy to upskill and reskill employees to be comfortable in using data. This goes without saying, but by establishing data literacy, the organization will know terminology, speak the same language, use common tools and technologies. Overall, data literacy helps to build the vocabulary and skills of the individuals in the workforce and establishes common methodologies.

Third, establish a data-driven decision-making culture and framework. When an organization is working towards common methodologies and techniques with regard to decision making, this will empower data fluency. Ensure your organization has a common framework it is utilizing towards data-driven decision making. If in this section our end goal is to establish data fluency, then using the same framework throughout the organization with regards to data-driven decision making can make it easier to see improvement in data fluency. This also establishes a process that is not haphazard, but is standard in the organization.

Fourth, ensure a strong onboarding process is in place to empower new hires and employees with the frameworks, strategy, and processes within data. This can help ensure the organization is not setting itself back with its new hire base. By establishing an onboarding process with regards to data, analytics, and literacy, then the culture and flow can continue.

Adaptability

For an organization's culture to succeed with data, it is imperative that the workforce is able to deal with the changing world and economies, the change in data tools and usage, etc. As was seen during the Covid-19 pandemic, organizations had to pull different levers, deal with different issues like virtual and remote work, try to deliver insights and results—so many different things. All of these things could be a hindrance to the work of a data-driven organization if the workforce is not strong, adaptable, and able to excel. If the workforce has the ability to "roll with the changes" then the organization can find ways to stay data driven in the face of unknown and different circumstances. How does a workforce become or stay adaptable?

This is complex and difficult to answer because it involves many moving parts. In the case of a data-driven organization, having a strong change management program, communication strategy, and continuous learning can empower adaptability. Having the right data literacy strategy gives the skills to be confident with data and the ever-changing needs therein. Overall, adaptability will empower the organization to be data driven as the workforce will be comfortable with the shifting times and needs of data and analytics.

One final note on adaptability: the leadership of the organization needs to set the example. As the organization deals with changes, the leadership must set the tone for the organizational culture as a whole on how it will utilize data and analytics to succeed and evolve through change.

Continuous learning

We have spoken much about learning throughout this book, and will still do so. For a culture to be data driven, the opportunities and chances for learning must be ever present. This isn't just a few licenses here and there with tools like Pluralsight, but it needs to be a strong investment with the company. As an organization, don't just say we want to provide the culture and workforce with opportunities to learn, show it.

Invest in organizational licenses for Pluralsight or another learning platform. Invest in focused learning time, where the workforce's calendars can be blocked, even for a short time, to invest in their learning. Build full learning programs and structures, especially with regards to how an organization can work and flow together from a data perspective.

One thought organizations should consider when it comes to a data literacy learning program is, does your organization have a data literacy lead? In my approaches to organizational learning, with some organizations we do a "train the trainer" approach, where the organization designates a person to lead data literacy in the organization. There is, in fact, a great company run by Valerie Logan that trains individuals and organizations to run a data literacy program.

The Data Lodge (The Data Lodge, 2021) is a unique program that allows organizations to take on data literacy programs in-house rather than having to hire a firm to run them. I find this to be a powerful way organizations can lead data literacy initiatives, learning to do it themselves versus having to continually hire organizations and firms to run the initiative for them. Valerie Logan—also known as the "Godmother of Data Literacy"—is one of the pioneering voices of data literacy in the world.

Other programs and organizations that provide data learning exist, enabling organizations to go to a library of content to learn. Herein, these programs require outside help with facilitating or a strong internal understanding of them, so they do not just become a place where individuals who aren't comfortable with data go and have to explore on their own to find the programs they want to use.

Finally, organizations and data and technology vendors, like Qlik or Tableau, provide learning both from a data literacy AND a tool perspective. This can be a powerful approach, empowering individuals in the moment to learn and grow within data and analytics.

To be data driven, organizations must have the mentality of continuous learning. Some may wish that they could just take a certificate course and arrive. Unfortunately, that will ultimately leave people and organizations behind. Again, the Covid-19 pandemic showed that organizations need to adapt and mold continuously. I am still amazed at how organizations had invested lots of money, but the pandemic opened their eyes to the gaps they were experiencing in data and analytics. Just throwing money at the tools and technologies, even investing in roles like chief data officer, didn't produce the magic necessary for success. True continuous learning in the organization is crucial. Invest in this wisely and don't hold back. The world of data is ever evolving and changing; don't let it run by as you miss opportunities here.

Diversified skill sets

Imagine you worked for an organization where all you hired for your data work were the exact same people and skill set. Even if that skill set were smart data scientists, do you think your organization would be as successful as it could be if you hired a set of diversified skills, allowing different viewpoints to come to light? We read from Grant and Rock (2016) that a more nuanced benefit of workplace diversity is that non-homogenous teams are smarter. Working with people from different backgrounds can challenge your brain into new ways of thinking and therefore improve its performance.

Bringing a diverse set of voices to your organization's data work is paramount. I have chatted with multiple people who didn't have a background within data and analytics who asked me, "Do I have a place here?" The answer is an emphatic yes! Everyone has a place at the data-driven table. In fact, I love having a diverse set of voices at the table of data and analytics because we need different minds, ideas, and thoughts to emerge. If everyone has the same background and ideas, we could be missing out on so many opportunities for more. We cannot become beholden to one set of skills and talent around data. This is a problem that needs to be addressed.

One example is a large financial services firm that came to me for help with its workforce. This organization had done what probably many organizations around the world had done: become enamored with this idea of data scientists. So, they had set out and hired data scientists throughout the organization and put them into each business unit. The only problem? The organization and business units didn't know how to utilize them. Each of these data scientists was probably very intelligent, but just hiring data scientists will not provide a coherent strategy and bring success. Instead, it was a case of hire and let the data scientists get to work. Thankfully, this organization started to pull away from this approach and started to build the center of excellence, to upskill and reskill the workforce. The approach became more strategic and intelligent. I now see this organization train interns regularly to understand the impact of data.

Another example of the diversifying of skills came to me by invitation. I received a message once from Columbia University in the United States. Through the conversation, I was invited to be a guest lecturer on communication to their master's degree program in statistics. This program did an excellent job of recognizing that there are other skills needed to prepare its students for the workforce. This is a great way to empower individuals to succeed in a career with data.

In fact, when I am asked by those in college who are getting degrees in statistics, data science, or a field along those lines, "what courses should I take?" I feel they are expecting me to tell them what courses within those fields they should take. That is not the answer I give. I tell them to diversify with skills in communication or leadership. The degrees will do enough to give you the technical skills. Instead, focus on other areas to become more well rounded as a data professional.

Now, I am also asked by those who have backgrounds in the arts or other areas if they have a place at the data and analytics table. The answer is absolutely, of course, yes! In fact, those who do not have a background in the STEM educations (science, technology, engineering and mathematics) have a powerful voice in data and analytics.

Why is that? One reason is because of the ability to see the full story, tell the story, or see the bigger picture. If you are a person with a background in the arts, utilize it as a strength within data and analytics. Use your ability to tell stories to your advantage. There is a reason it is no longer just STEM education, but STEAM education. I have been wanting the arts to be a part of it for a long time, and I am glad it has happened.

Overall, having diverse voices is a powerful way to get more insight, to see things from a different perspective, to potentially eliminate biases, and to have more voices at the table. If you are in leadership, look to your workforce and understand if you have diversified voices. Have a culture of continuous learning and adaptability to bring all the voices to the table.

Growth vs fixed mindset

These two terms really came into vogue with the book by Carol Dweck: *Mindset: The new psychology of success*. From the website *Mindset Health* we read: "A growth mindset means that you believe your intelligence and talents can be developed over time. A fixed mindset means that you believe intelligence is fixed—so if you're not good at something, you might believe you'll never be good at it" (Smith, 2020). As you can see here, part of the issue lies in our mindsets. Within a data-driven culture, the organization needs to take on the personality of a growth mindset versus a fixed mindset.

Here, we turn back to our change management, continuous learning, and so forth. It is understood that not everyone is the same, not everyone is going to have the same talents, abilities, and not everyone will have the same mindset. But what we want to build throughout the organization is an ability and mindset that are growing, open, and able to learn and develop. Within the world of data and analytics, one can see that a fixed mindset might lead individuals to resist the overall tools, technologies, data literacy programs, etc. How can we overcome a fixed mindset and empower the workforce to be able to have a growth mindset? You can find many different answers to that question with a simple Google search. Here, I want to touch upon two areas that will empower the organization to be data driven by putting in place improvements and help. These areas come as a set of steps or processes that can help drive the growth mindset (Scott, 2021):

1 Know the organization's "learning style"—what does that even mean? Depending on your role or position, when the leadership of an organization knows the learning style of the organization, how it develops, the talents and skills, it can have an easier time implementing changes and more. By knowing the various methodologies that will work within your organization, the various skills, the cultural aspects of the organization (those beliefs and such), the organization can implement correct learning and programs. This can help the growth vs fixed mindset. If you look to implement standard learning-type solutions or new technologies without much transparency, you may not get strong results. Ensure everyone feels involved, that their thoughts and processes are addressed.

2 Cultivate a sense of purpose—when your organization's workforce feels it has a purpose with regards to being data driven, your organization can get behind the work, evolutions, and changes that take place as your organization becomes more successful with data-driven work. If individuals do not feel a part of something, if they are not behind the programs, strategies, and work you are doing with data, they may feel "fixed" and more like it is a forced program. When individuals in the workforce feel that the work you are doing from a data and analytics perspective has meaning, when they feel a part of it, then it can be easier for implementing this work going forward.

It can be easy to see why a growth mindset can help an organization succeed and why a fixed mindset can be a hindrance. From a data-driven culture perspective, establish the personality of the organization to be growth minded. Easier said than done. What if the leadership that wants a growth mindset has a fixed mindset? What if you have your own fixed mindset? Cultivate a growth mindset within the organization, its leadership, and yourself.

Gamification and reward-based systems

The idea of gamification is not new, but I feel it has gained a lot of steam within organizations around the world of data and analytics over the past few years. Gamification is like it sounds—we are going to "gamify" data and analytics. One of the most common ways I hear about this happening is through a badging system. What do I mean by a badging system?

In careers, individuals are looking for ways to distinguish themselves. A "badge" for data and analytics is a way to help individuals aspire to something that can be attached to their resume. This can be especially helpful for those who do not have a background in data and analytics. If we are able to put a badge or certificate behind their names, we can help them understand the development, the growth, make their resume shine more, etc. I have been asked about the badging and gamification of data literacy and the skills associated with a data-driven organization many times.

On top of the badging system, rewards-based systems are a way to motivate, help with a growth mindset, and help the organization recognize employees as they move forward. As you implement learning strategies, you can implement rewards-based approaches as individuals complete tasks, learning, and so forth. You can also implement rewards-based systems as you complete projects and see successful work within the data and analytics community internal to your organization.

The utilization of gamification and rewards-based systems is a way to also involve areas of organizations that usually may not feel they are that involved in data and analytics. For example, historically, the human resources area may not have felt a part of the data and analytics work. I can tell you that I do a lot of work within organizations and the human resources area to drive data-driven approaches. Utilizing a rewards-based system, the gamification of the organization, can help areas of the business feel a part of a data-driven strategy. Also note that you should use data and information to establish your gamification and rewards-based system. Don't just say "this is what we are doing," but establish a data-driven approach to understand how your organization would like to be rewarded. Assuming what will work can be a difficult road for success within this. Find out the personality of the organization to understand how it would like to be rewarded. This will take effort, but it will allow the organization to understand its personality more and more, and then allow it to take a data-driven approach to rewards.

Embrace failure

Organizations around the world will use catchy phrases like "fail fast" or "fail fast and learn" or something along these lines. Unfortunately, what I have found is that a lot of organizations use these phrases but they do not truly embrace them. There is fear in organizations of a projection failing. There is fear of something having an 85 percent chance of success and not working. The world of a data-driven organization, one using data and analytics for operation and decision making, is one that will have failure and iterations ongoing.

Organizational culture for a data-driven organization needs to be one where failure is celebrated or utilized for learning. Nelson Mandela said, "I never lose. I either win or learn" (Goodreads, 2021). This quote has power in the world of a data-driven organization and culture. Statistics is a field that is based on probabilities. With probabilities, things will fail, even if we find a 90 percent chance of something happening. For example, imagine you are an organization that has built a study around workforce retention and a new program designed to abate the attrition in your organization. Through a data-driven approach, you find the likelihood of this program succeeding to be around 85 percent. That number is high and seems like good odds for you and your organization.

As you implement the program, you find something else is happening. You find that not only has attrition not slowed down, but it has sped up a little bit. You sit and stew over this in your mind: "Wow, could something with an 85 percent chance of success not work?" What we fail to realize sometimes is that with an 85 percent chance of something working, there is a 15 percent chance that it won't. In the case of your organization's new retention program, we found the 15 percent. Is this a bad thing? Not necessarily. Herein we must learn to embrace failure and follow the quote by Nelson Mandela. It is not failure that occurred, but a learning opportunity.

In the real world, we may all be familiar with things like this that occur on a regular basis: political elections. In political elections we see candidates with a strong likelihood of winning. In some cases, one candidate is predicted to have a very high likelihood of winning. Then, election night comes around and the candidate with the favorable odds ends up not winning. How can this be? Well, again, there is the flip side to that "odds of winning." In some cases, maybe the prediction was made poorly. Maybe the statistics were flawed. In some cases, the odds just fall out of favor.

Organizational work is going to be the same. Instead of a mindset that something "has to" or "must" work, especially given strong odds, we must develop an iterative mindset. Data and analytics is like an eternal circle. You start something, go through the process of analyzing it and making a decision, then you study the decision, learn from it, and start again; it is a perpetual cycle. This is the essence of embracing failure. Your culture is good when an individual works on a project, thinks that the direction it is going in is a good one, only to learn it isn't. Truly learn to embrace failure, utilize it as a learning opportunity, and this can empower your organization's culture to succeed with data. If they fear failure or the repercussions when something doesn't go right, then it can be a roadblock to your goal of being data driven.

Clear vision and strategy

We do not need to belabor this point, as we have spoken on strategy in this book already. For an organization's culture to be data driven, where data and analytics is embraced, does your workforce have a clear understanding of the vision and strategy your organization is taking with data? You may feel like your organization has a good grasp, but based on my experience, the answer is likely that they do not.

I have spoken to companies all over the world and at many events. In my travels and opportunities to speak, I have found the trend to be that most individuals in an organization, even the data professionals, do not have a clear understanding of what your organization is trying to do with data and analytics. This in turn means they do not necessarily know how the work they are doing is furthering the business strategy.

Without a succinct and sound understanding in your organization of what the intended goals and strategies with data are, how can the culture flourish? Ensure your organization has set in place the sound principles of transparency, communication, and a clear understanding by the employees of their role in the strategy.

I fear many companies feel or have adopted, whether knowingly or not, the idea that data and analytics should be like an easy button. You invest in the tools, you source the data, and boom, you have a magic button that should drive a data-driven business. Unfortunately, this is not the case. In the world of data and analytical strategy and vision, take the time to build this properly. More time spent upfront helps empower the long-term future. Through that work, ensure the rest of the organization knows what is happening with data. This means for all employees, whether they have the word "data" in their title or not. Ensure the culture understands in totality the roles and things happening in the organization.

Grassroots

How should your organization become data driven? Is it done through a top-down approach? Is it done through a bottom-up, grassroots mentality? The reality and answer to that question is actually that it is both. We have devoted a lot of time to the leadership of the organization; let's now turn to the grassroots movements that can occur in data and analytics to drive this success.

Collins Dictionary (2021) indicate that when referring to organizations or movements, the "grassroots" are the people within it, not the leaders. A grassroots movement or work is done through the workforce and is not the charge of its leaders. I worked with an organization where the movement to being more data literate was done with a small sub-group of employees.

This organization had over 100,000 employees overall, but can you guess the size of the working group I helped drive data literacy with? Only 150 employees in total. These employees were hand-picked, a smaller subsection of some who 1) their leaders thought would be a good addition, or 2) were excited about data. Essentially, we were creating an internal army of data literacy evangelists for the organization to succeed with. We were using the organization's employees to gain enthusiasm and build an "army" to succeed, to be more data driven and data literate.

For your organization and mine, the reality is you need enthusiasm from the employee ranks for a data-driven culture to thrive and for a data-driven organization to succeed. If the mandate only comes from the top down and the workforce doesn't feel it has the support or power of the organization's employees behind it, then the data-driven approach can be greatly hindered. Through the workforce, find those who are enthusiastic about data and analytics and get them to help you.

One key area where you can help to create a voice and movement from a grassroots perspective is through a "data and analytics community." We can see some of these communities exist through different tool vendors like Tableau and Alteryx. Each of these data and analytical tools has a strong community backing them for success. A community like these, but in our case internal to the organization, helps to design a space for employees to collaborate, work together, and have open dialogue around data and analytical topics. These communities should not be solely for data scientists or those with "data" in their professional title. Instead, these should be internal, social networks that allow everyone, from every background, to come together and share ideas, thoughts, questions, concerns, and anything else that can help the organization to be data driven.

These communities are not hard to get going. For many organizations, you can start them through your internal messaging apps. For example, in my current organization, you can find "communities" through our company's Slack app. There are different communities and channels, such as one on meditation. For the company of over 100,000 employees, utilizing a system like Slack or Microsoft Teams was our answer to help facilitate a community. Allow employees to join these channels, create them to be fun and engaging, helping all to feel welcome to the data and analytical table, regardless of background.

There are other things that can be done to help facilitate the grassroots movement. Have guest speakers come and deliver webinar-type meetings, almost like a TED Talk, to help share inspiration or motivation around data and analytics. Hold office hours with data professionals, so the employees have a place to turn that allows them to ask open questions. Making these open spaces allows more participation. If one person has a particular question, it might be that another has that same question.

Allowing these office hours, communities, and more allows for learning to take place; a community can grow, and the enthusiasm can flow like a grassroots movement. If it is just a mandate that comes down from leadership, I am not sure you will find the success you want. But by making the overall program more culture- and organization-wide, finding the grassroots in your organization can help facilitate more success.

Recognition of biases

Unfortunately, this one chapter is not here to be the golden ticket that helps to root out the systemic biases that can creep into data and analytical work. Let's make sure we understand what is meant by biases from a data and analytical perspective. Bias in data and analytics is where the data and information we find, present, or communicate has a bias away from the expected results or a systemic issue within the data that skews results and outcomes. In this case, there are systemic biases, there are human biases, and there are just plain choices made with data and analytics that can skew the results away from the expected norms and outcomes.

Is it possible to rid an organization of all biases? Of course not! The key is the recognition of biases in an organization and how to deal with them. Remember, we are not speaking of the straight biases and prejudices that can be found in society; rather we are speaking of the biases that can be systemic to our processes in a data-driven culture and organization. Two common forms of biases in data and analytics are:

- *Confirmation bias*: This is an error that involves allowing a preconceived notion to impact how you prioritize or interpret information. An example of confirmation bias would be if you had a strong opinion that most people preferred vanilla ice cream over chocolate ice cream and, as a result, gave more weight to data that supported that conclusion (Mailchimp, 2021).

- *Selection bias*: This is an error that stems from using population samples that don't accurately represent the entire target group. For example, data taken from one neighborhood would not accurately represent a large city. There are many reasons selection bias arises— some intentional, some not—including voluntary participation, limiting factors for participation, or insufficient sample size (Mailchimp, 2021).

The key to having a data-driven organization is not to try to get rid of biases altogether at once, as that is just trying to boil the ocean. Instead, in a data-driven culture and organization, the goal is to recognize them, help put systems in place that can help alleviate the outcome and problems of biases, provide training for the recognition of biases, and so forth.

As you can imagine, an entire book can be written on the world of biases within data and analytics. To try to rid the organization of issues within biases altogether is a massive task. Instead, for your data-driven culture, put training and processes in place to help employees recognize, encounter, and account for the biases. Over time, with these processes in place and a more data-literate organization, hopefully you will find your organizational data biases are waning away and you are finding more success with your data-driven goals.

Conclusion

I will continue to say over and over again that the number one roadblock to data and analytical success in an organization is its culture. With all the beliefs, traditions, experiences, different skill sets, the personality of the organization, all of these things lead to the need to establish a strong data-driven culture. In this chapter we have covered several key points to line up a data-driven culture. Those points were:

- data fluency
- adaptability
- continuous learning
- diversified skill sets
- growth vs fixed mindset
- gamification and reward-based systems
- embracing failure
- clear vision and strategy
- grassroots
- recognition of biases

These are just pillars or characteristics of a data-driven organization when they are properly put in place. Not one of these characteristics in a stand-alone perspective will get the work done. Neither can an organization just put in place tools, technologies, or say "hey, this data area looks like it is going to be big," and hope for success. Instead, look to your workforce, design learning paths for success. Find the diversified voices and mindsets. Empower your employees with the clear vision and path. Reward them for their work. Rid yourselves of or recognize your biases. If needed, find programs that can help you, like Pluralsight's online learning platform or Valerie Logan's Data Lodge, which empowers organizations to lead their own data literacy journey.

Overall, your organization's culture will be a key to your success. Create a data-driven culture, empower your workforce, and your data-driven success can be even greater!

PART THREE

Building your data-driven organization

In this final section, we will help you build your data-driven organization.

9

Decide your outcome

Throughout this book so far, we have delved into two parts: Part One, chapters 1 through 4, focused on foundational thoughts. Part Two, chapters 5 through 8, focused on skills gaps. It is time now for us to focus on the third part: how do we build a data-driven organization? In Chapter 9, we are going to discuss what I call the first step or where you start: your outcome.

To do this, I am going to start with a personal example from my life. When we think of data and analytical work, sometimes it can be a monumental task, something overwhelming and hard. I liken it to ultra-marathons, a task I love to take on but which is mind- and gut-wrenching at times in its magnitude. But, like anything else, it must start with that single first step. Let me walk through a thought process for an ultra-marathon, then tie that to your outcomes. We can then explore different outcomes your organization can start with and how creating a library of successful data-driven outcomes can help shape and motivate your organization.

Before jumping in, please know that even though the task can seem monumental and too hard to complete, just know it can be done. It can take time to do it right. It may mean you eliminate work that has been done for a long time. It may mean recognition that some investments in the past were the wrong investments. But, like we said in the last chapter, embrace failure and learn. Overall, if you build a data-driven organization correctly, you can succeed now and into the future. This is not hyperbole or overstating: it is fact.

The ultra-marathon

"You are crazy" is a usual statement when an individual finds out I run ultra-marathons. I find ultra-marathons to be like the data journey itself, but please know, even though an ultra-marathon has a "finish line," the race isn't over just because you cross it—you set out to tackle another and then another. The race is never over, it is a life-long pursuit. The same needs to be said about data and analytics. An organization is data driven when it continually works to be data driven. You will not find the "finish line" and be able to sit back and call it "done."

For background, an ultra-marathon is a race that is greater than the marathon distance of 26.2 miles. Usually, the starting distance for an ultra-marathon is 50k, or around 31.1 miles. One other thing to note is that most ultra-marathons are run on trails and not on the road. I myself am a trail runner and love to be in the mountains; the distance is just a piece of the entire puzzle, it isn't the puzzle itself. Let me explain.

When I look at ultra-marathons, I want to set out to find a true outcome for the races I finish, but it isn't just that. I have new outcomes and desires when I set out to do a race. With my first ultra-marathon, my outcome was to just finish. When taking on such a distance, just finishing is a monumental and fun thing. With other races, the outcome can become something altogether different. For example, let me share a few examples of races I have taken on and my process and thinking for the outcomes:

- *The Pony Express 50 Miler* (second time). In this race, my desired outcome was a speedy 50 miles. This race did not have much vertical gain, so it was relatively flat. I wanted to push the pace on this one. Something occurred in the race that changed my trajectory and my outcome: my right knee flared up, causing pain and issues. So, for the second half of the race, I adjusted and changed the desired outcome. It was a successful race.

- *The Speedgoat 50k.* This is rated one of the hardest ultra-marathons in the world, not because of the distance but because of the steep and difficult climbing. This race has anywhere from 11,000 to 14,000 feet of vertical gain during the race. When I raced it for the first time, it was just the thought process of finishing—that was the desired outcome. The second time I raced it, I had to adjust my outcome because the race broke me mentally.

- *The Leadville 100.* This is my favorite race in the world. The desired outcome was just to plain finish. An infection before the race caused some trepidation, but I set out. Unfortunately, the infection hurt me more than we knew it would and the outcome wasn't what I wanted, but with this race, as with all others, there are daily outcomes.

Ultra-marathons require a different mentality that needs to be taken on to set out to try them. One thing to note about the races, though, is that you set a final outcome, what you want to accomplish through the race, but you also set smaller duration outcomes: What do I want to accomplish in my training today? This week? This month? What about my nutrition, what do I need to do with my nutrition outcome to be successful? All of these things need to have their own outcomes to ensure proper training and success.

The ultra-marathon as the data-driven organization

As you can imagine, the stories of my races above can easily be tied as metaphors to the data-driven world. We should have large outcomes at the end, but small, manageable wins and goals, steps to get us there. At times, our outcomes will have to shift based on varying conditions, internal and external aspects. There are many things the ultra-marathon racing world can be likened to within a data-driven business. How do you figure out these different outcomes? What can you do to tie this type of thinking back to the business world and being data driven? What steps can you take to determine your outcome for data? Here are the steps you should use to determine your outcomes in being data driven:

- *Get the right people involved.* Do you have the right personnel in place to set the outcome? Do they have the right skills?

- *Hold planning meetings.* Set in place planning meetings. Note: these should not be all-day meetings, where you are locked in a room for eight hours straight, working through lunch. We will speak about the effectiveness of meetings and setting the right tone.

- *Understand your current situation.* Do you know your current data-driven situation? Do you have the landscape in place? What are the skills of the organization? What tools and technologies do you have?

- *Establish the "why."* Do you know your "why" behind doing these things? Are you just doing something because you read about it online, heard about it from a peer or colleague, or are you doing it just because you think it should be done? Know your why!

- *Know your business strategy inside and out.* Do you have a good grasp on what the business is trying to do? If you are a leader, do you know what you truly want to accomplish as a business? If you are an employee, do you understand what your business is doing and your role in it? Hint: a lot of employees may not truly know this, so this is very important.

- *Do not boil the ocean.* Are you trying to take on too much within the business and data? If you are not a very data-driven company right now, can you start off by setting small outcomes and creating a library of wins? Hint: this can be a great way to set the tone for your business.

- *Set your outcome statement and vision.* Do you have an outcome statement and vision that is set and then shared throughout the organization? Is this top of people's minds as they work with data? Have you had each business unit and area set out smaller outcome statements that roll up into the overall outcome statement? (Chapman, 2020)

These processes for helping you determine your outcome goals within data and analytics, to be data driven, will empower your organization to succeed with data. By solving each one of these, you will be able to then set a strategy in place, but more on that in the next chapter. Let's dive into each one of these areas and share thoughts on them, what you can do, and how to empower your organization to be outcome driven with data and analytics.

Get the right people involved

To help you determine your outcome and what you want to accomplish, having the right people in place is of paramount importance; voices at the table matter. For example, as I run ultra-marathons and look to set the outcomes I want to accomplish in the various races I am trying to finish, I am inviting those to my table who can truly help me set the right outcome. For ultra-marathons, it can be inviting those who I train with, or those who have finished the races, getting to know new people who are familiar with the race and can help achieve the right expectation and understanding. It may be that I hire a coach (something we will talk about shortly) who knows the race, gets to know me and my goals, etc., who can then put in place true outcomes and not some outlandish thought process I may have in mind.

Within your organization, as you set out to determine your desired outcome with data, have the right people in place. Use your data and analytics leadership to start the process, and this should take you all the way to the C-suite of the organization. Ensure the CEO is aware of what is happening. Ensure you get diverse voices from within the data organization to opine on the outcomes once in draft form. Sometimes we can set an outcome in place, but we don't involve enough voices throughout the organization to share if the outcome we are looking for is even possible. Let me share an example of an organization that was setting out on a data literacy initiative, but it did not seem like the right people were at the table to establish the outcomes and strategies for the program: I will share why.

Isolated groups

I was working with a financial organization that had a lot of motivation from one group to really become data literate, empowering a data-driven organization. There was enthusiasm, and the ideas they shared seemed to be great ideas. There was a big problem, though. It appeared this group was in a silo, it was isolated. As I spoke to them, it was clear that they didn't know what the organization was trying to do with data. The group knew they wanted to be more data literate, but they didn't know the outcomes for data and the strategy that was being put in place. In essence, this group was motivated, excited, and doing a lot of work to build this program, but they didn't have the seat at the table of understanding. They were not aware of the overall data strategy. The motivation and ideas were strong, but the process was flawed in that this group was not involved or at the table to understand the data-driven goals of the organization; they just knew they wanted this program.

Now, you may say, at least the company was doing something, trying something, and you would be right. Yes, they at least were doing something, which for some organizations is not the case. The problem was, this group didn't have a clear understanding of what was happening, so instead of knowing if the direction they were taking was correct, the cart was in front of the horse. By not having a seat at the "outcome table," their program may have led the organization in wrong directions or the work may not have benefited the learners as much as it could have, had it been designed to help workers tie back to the outcome.

Having the right people at the meetings is essential. As you look to establish your outcomes, work with a diverse set of voices to ensure you are working properly. How do you know who should be at the table? Allow the chief data officer or the leader in charge of data to determine. You need to allow enough voices to opine on the situation, but not too many, because you can then slow your pace down to possibly even less than that of a snail. Just ensure you have not only leaders giving their thoughts, but also workers from within data and analytics. Why?

By having workers within the data and analytics space at the table to discuss what outcomes you want with data, they can share their views and thoughts on what would work and what wouldn't. Sometimes, we can become so visionary that we don't see the forest for the trees. Meaning, our eyes can become so big and so excited around being data driven, we can miss something and then set ourselves back or slow the process. Allow voices to come in, allow dissenting voices, and arrive at a truly data-driven outcome for your organization.

Hold planning meetings

Those that know me, know I do not like ineffective meetings. Far too often, meetings are held for meetings' sake. Meetings give us a feeling of accomplishment, that we actually did something and we can check it off. But when you think about it, how many of our meetings truly accomplish something? How much "fluff" and ineffective work was done in the meeting? Do you feel your meetings around data are effective? Far too often, I hear complaints, dissenting voices that yet again a meeting wasn't effective.

How often do you have long meetings scheduled on your calendar? How about all-day meetings? Have you ever had to sit through a two-hour meeting, where you just "pushed through"? In this case, did you know you weren't being very data driven? Data will show that the effectiveness of the meeting decreases as the length of the meeting increases (MeetingKing, 2015). For meetings to determine your outcome, I subscribe to the 30-minute meeting or less. It is fine to hold multiple meetings, but overall the brain's capacity dwindles over time.

Meeting tools

To ensure the effectiveness of these data-driven outcome meetings, ensure you prepare a strong and powerful agenda (MeetingKing, 2015). Send out pre-reads to make sure the attendees know what they are getting themselves into. Using pre-reads can eliminate wasteful time in the beginning of the meeting by giving people backgrounds. The agenda and pre-read should empower every participant with the knowledge and understanding of what the meeting is for, why they are attending, and then set an outcome for the meeting (yes, set a meeting outcome to help determine the desired outcome for your organization's data).

One final note or two about meetings. Albert Einstein is attributed as saying: "If you can't explain it to a six-year-old, you don't understand it yourself" (Bornhofen, 2021). Within our context, if you cannot explain to a six-year-old why you are holding these meetings, do not set them up. People's time is precious. Ensure you are fully prepared to hold the meetings that take place. If you are to attend a planning meeting for a data-driven outcome, ensure you can explain your role and your purpose there. Doing so can help make these meetings more effective.

The second note on meetings comes to us from Elon Musk, whose rules for meetings I truly love (Haden, 2021):

- *Stop holding large meetings.* You don't need everyone at the table, just the right people.

- *Stop holding frequent meetings.* You do not need to waste people's time. Again, holding meetings does not mean you are doing effective data-driven work, it may just mean you are holding frequent meetings. Make them effective, not frequent.

- *Feel free to walk out of meetings.* If you find yourself in a meeting and you do not find you need to be there, then yes, you can walk out. Provide an explanation and then get to work.

- *Stop using acronyms and buzzwords.* The world of data and analytics is full of buzzwords. Stop using them! Using buzzwords doesn't mean someone knows what they are talking about. If you don't know what something is, raise your hand. Use real, concrete language and leave the acronyms at the door.

- *Stop following the (communication) chain of command.* I love this rule very much. You don't have to follow the chain of command for every communication. In Elon's rules, go the shortest distance to get things done. If you are invited to a data-driven outcome meeting, then you can voice directly to those in charge—you don't have to go through various bodies to be heard.

- *Stop limiting communication between departments.* Communication needs to be open and transparent. As you look to establish your data-driven outcome, communication should be free flowing, especially because your organization's outcome will span across teams and departments. Keep all those lines of communication open. This can prevent teams from being left behind and silos from occurring.

- *Stop following stupid rules.* This is another gem. Get things out of the way that are going to prevent you from establishing your outcome. If you feel something is a stupid rule and it is preventing your meeting from being effective or you are finding it is getting in the way of establishing a strong data-driven outcome, then voice your opinion and see if everyone can move on from it.

I think all of us have been to one, some, or many meetings we felt were very ineffective. To be productive with data, limit the length and frequency of meetings. Use time wisely, take advantage of pre-reads and getting voices to the table. To establish your data-driven outcome, use meetings effectively and not just to feel good about doing something.

Understand your current situation

How can you set an outcome without knowing where you currently are? While yes, it is true you can set an aspirational outcome and attack it from that perspective, the reality is, you need to do an assessment to understand your current situation and to help establish an outcome. If you are a leader, you should know the skills of the organization, the personality, the culture, and tools and technologies that you currently have present throughout the workforce. As a leader, you should know what kind of return you are getting already on your data work, as I presume pretty much every organization around the world is using some data and information to do their work; even small, locally owned businesses are using the information and data they know to make decisions. Each organization and business should understand its current situation to help drive outcomes.

Consultancies

Herein comes an opportunity to hire outside consultancies to help drive and understand the work and the situation your organization finds itself in. Remember, put in the right amount of work at the front end of your data-driven organizational work to help support the long future. I fear that far too often we want quick, easy, and powerful decisions to come from data, but this is not the reality. In this case, an outside consultancy can help to set the tone from a third-party perspective, helping you either as a leader or employee to understand your current situation and any limitations that may arise, and this can help you to set a good outcome. Then, once that outcome is finished, just like from one ultra-marathon to the next, you set out with the next outcome. For example, one organization I was recruited to work for was looking to bring me in to help build out its self-service analytics. This organization is probably well known as a "data-driven" organization, but the data and systems were a mess. At the time, I was the outside party. While I took another job instead, the outcome would have probably started out as cleaning up those systems and messes, then I could have built out the self-service capabilities. I could have come in as an outside factor, cleaned up one outcome, and gotten to the next. I would have been able to understand the situation, see the forest for the trees, and put plans in place.

Utilize the right assessments, tools, and people to help you understand and establish what your current data-driven situation is and the gaps and problems that may persist. Then, with this information in mind, you are more prepared to understand the possible outcomes you can achieve. Just like assessing my skills and abilities for the race, even bringing in a coach, can help me set the reality of my outcomes and situation, the same can be said of establishing that vision for a data-driven organization.

Establish the "why"

I think we hear this over and over again, but the reality is, repetition can bring success. Unfortunately, I come across many organizations that have not established the why of the data outcome. If you want to be data driven, ensure your organization is set to succeed with data by the workforce having a solid understanding of the why.

The "why" of data and analytics is a major part of your outcome. Imagine you are an advertising firm, looking to utilize data to drive more successful advertising campaigns. That is the outcome your organization is trying to succeed with, your data outcome. The why is to help the organization generate more revenue to build out an expansion into four key markets. Here, we have the outcome and the why. Imagine you are a private equity firm that is trying to utilize data to increase the profitability of your organizational investments (note: this can take on many forms as this could be data utilization in many facets of the business)—the outcome. Now, establish the why: you want to increase the profitability of your organizational investments for reasons x, y, and z. Again, here we know the outcome and we know the why. Share your organization's outcome and why, helping the workforce to be prepared.

Now, the question may be, what do we start with—the outcome or the why? The why should be an established part of your business. Your organization's workforce will have, or at least should have, good ideas about your vision and what you want to accomplish, but more importantly should know why you want to accomplish it. The why will be a pre-established thing in your organization. We will start with that. The outcome for your data-driven organization will then be built on the why.

As you then communicate out your why, which we will talk about more in our next chapter, please understand that the business will own and maintain the overarching why, whereas the different business units and groups will establish their own whys. Each business unit and department has its work to achieve strategies and outcomes, so setting their own whys is important, as long as they tie back to the overarching why. Now, what does a bad example of a why look like?

Bad why

I worked with a financial organization, large, established, over 100 years old, that was enamored, as were many organizations, with the thought of data science. Why not, right? We have heard of the power of data science for a long time. Unfortunately, the outcome and why were not established well in this organization. They hired many data scientists, in each of the business units, expecting success and good work with data and analytics. Unfortunately, the data scientists were not utilized well, if at all, and the organization had spent many dollars but not received the ROI. This was mainly because they were not working towards a clearly defined why or outcome. With a why, these data scientists could have been used to achieve the outcome. With a why, they could have known why they were doing the work. Ensure your organization uses a why to truly be data driven.

Know your business strategy inside and out

This may seem intuitive and necessary, but notice I did not title this part of the work "know your data strategy." In your current role, whether as a data leader, other leader, or different role in the organization, your job is to know your business strategy inside and out. This should be something every employee in an organization is looking to do, but to help you and your organization know what your data-driven outcome should be, know your strategy.

The question can become, can I have more than one data-driven outcome? Yes, the answer to this is yes. Depending on the data maturity of your organization, having more than one outcome is ok. The key is to, well, follow the things this book has put forward: know your change management strategy, know your workforce's skills, know your culture. Many things to know here. When you are in the depths of your organizational strategy, with a sound understanding of your organization's BUSINESS outcome, you can then put forth your organization's DATA outcome. Data is a support valve and system for your business strategy to succeed. End of sentence, final point, done. This is the purpose of your data outcome, to help you drive forward with your business strategy and to push in a successful way.

As a part of your organization's learning on your business strategy, ensure you have built out clear-cut communications and plans. With strong communication, dissemination of information, and overall work, you and your workforce can be in a strong position to succeed with a data-driven outcome.

Do not boil the ocean

There is so much work to be done towards a data-driven outcome and business. There is the gathering of data correctly and having it stored correctly. There is the right business intelligence, empowering the workforce to make the right data-driven decisions. The right culture and plan need to be in place. You can ask yourself the following questions: Do I have the right hiring practices? Have I chosen the right data outcome? Am I in a position to lead an organization, team, or individually within data? There are so many questions, so many things to be done, etc. The reality is, you do not need to do it all at once. In fact, if you try to do that, you may set yourself back, burn out, not accomplish much, or find yourself in a worse position than you were before. Do not try to boil the ocean.

Step by step

Instead of boiling the ocean and trying to do too much, take it step by step. Like me with an ultra-marathon, I may have set my outcome to be to finish this race or that race, but the reality is there will be many things that need to be done to hit that outcome. I will have one overarching outcome of finishing the race, but then many outcomes that help along the way: daily training, daily nutrition, the right gear, the right plan, etc. There are many outcomes that help me to achieve the big outcome.

Do the same with data-driven outcomes. You will have your one large outcome, and then set some outcomes along the way to becoming a truly data-driven organization. In this case, this means taking the time to prioritize the right outcome, the right thing to accomplish first. With the right understanding of your workforce, capabilities, and more, you will be able to then assess the right priority. Is it to move all your data to the Cloud? Is it to establish strong democratization of data with the right business intelligence tool? Is it establishing the right data literacy learning program to start? You will be able to figure this out, to determine what to do.

One benefit of this type of staggered or "one thing at a time" approach to becoming data driven and establishing your outcomes is that it can create proof points to success. I get asked often, how do I get people onboard with data and analytics? By creating different outcomes and accomplishing them, you are creating a library of successes that prove the value of data. This can then be used as a demonstration to those still on the fence. Use your library of outcome proof points to drive home the success of data and analytics.

Set your outcome and vision statement

A vision statement should have the ability to inspire and motivate others around a concept or idea. It can establish a benchmark, provide line of sight, direction, and where the organization wants to be in a set period of years. The purpose of setting a vision is twofold: firstly, it is there to create a long-term strategy for where the company is going; secondly, it is meant to align everyone around the company's direction. A vision should establish something on the horizon that is out of our comfort zone, challenging us to stretch ourselves while being somewhat attainable. It should clearly indicate the direction in which you want to move. This allows others to invest in the future with an understanding of their purpose as an employee. (Meyer-Cuno, 2021)

In our careers, we have all probably heard a vision statement or about the importance of having one. When you have determined your outcome for your data and analytics, whether the large overarching outcome for the company or the smaller outcomes for the teams and other areas of the organization, set a vision statement that opens up the organization to move forward.

As the quote above states, the vision statement should inspire and motivate people in the workforce. It should set the direction for the outcome-driven approach to data. Let this statement be bold, empowering, and strong for your workforce and organization to succeed with your data outcome.

Conclusion

Overall, the first step in your data-driven approach as an organization is to set the outcome. To help you drive the outcome, remember our pillars:

- *Get the right people involved.* Do you have the right personnel in place to set the outcome? Do they have the right skills?

- *Hold planning meetings.* Set in place planning meetings. Note: these should not be all-day meetings, where you are locked in a room for eight hours straight, working through lunch.

- *Understand your current situation.* Do you know your current data-driven situation? Do you have the landscape in place? What are the skills of the organization? What tools and technologies do you have?

- *Establish the "why."* Do you know your "why" behind doing these things? Are you just doing something because you read about it online, heard about it from a peer or colleague, or are you doing it just because you think it should be done? Know your why!

- *Know your business strategy inside and out.* Do you have a good grasp on what the business is trying to do? If you are a leader, do you know what you truly want to accomplish as a business? If you are an employee, do you understand what your business is doing and your role in it? Hint: a lot of employees may not truly know this, so this is very important.

- *Do not boil the ocean.* Are you trying to take on too much within the business and data? If you are not a very data-driven company right now, can you start off by setting small outcomes and creating a library of wins? Hint: this can be a great way to set the tone for your business.

- *Set your outcome statement and vision.* Do you have an outcome statement and vision that is set and then shared throughout the organization? Is this top of people's minds as they work with data? Have you had each business unit and area set out smaller outcome statements that roll up into the overall outcome statement? (Chapman, 2020)

With the outcome in place, with you comfortable now on how to set your data-driven outcome, it is time to understand how to build a strategy around your outcome. Please note, we will move through the pillars above for setting your strategy. You will find that these pillars are uniform and can empower your overall data-driven organization.

10

Build your strategy

With your outcome in place, you can now set out to build your data-driven strategy; you now have a direction you can take when moving forward. That is the key. Historically, companies may use a technology or something dealing with a technology as their strategy, which is not a strategy. For example, if you invest money in a business intelligence tool like Power BI or Tableau, then you may have said "Tableau is our strategy." That is not a strategy. The tool is an enabler of your strategy. With the outcome ready, you now have a targeted direction, your compass. Now, it is time to set the plans, strategies, goals, and motions in place to achieve that direction and head towards what you can call your company's "North Star."

There are many wonderful books on strategy in the business world, even in the data strategy world, with Bernard Marr's great book *Data Strategy*. We will approach the data-driven strategy from a different perspective. We covered multiple pillars within the previous chapter and we will bring in pillars to building your strategy and the essential elements each data-driven strategy should possess. That said, of course there will be variations from the outcome pillars. Then, we will look at the application of those different areas, with examples of how to drive those points home within your data-driven strategy. We will transition to a three-point cycle that you can use with your strategy to ensure it is working: Goal to Action to Recycle. Finally, we will use cases from my work with companies to set in place examples and proof points or ideas of what you and your organization can do to truly become a data-driven organization.

Ultra-marathon strategy

For our purposes, let's dive back into my ultra-marathon running to bring to light what I mean when I say now that the outcome is in place, you can set the strategy. Within ultra-running, each race is a different animal. When going those long distances, you have different outcomes, ideas, and thoughts about how you want to finish the race. I was asked after I finished a certain race, what would the next goal be? This is the outcome stage. Let me pick an example of a race that I have on my mind: the Speedgoat 50k. This race is rated one of the hardest in the world, with around 11,000–12,000 feet of vertical gain, and much of it more than 9,000 feet above sea level. This race is in July, it is hot, and you are exposed a lot during the race. Let's just say it hurts. I think I really want to push and determine a speedy outcome to finish that race: sub-seven hours. OK, I have the outcome set at sub-seven hours, now what do I do? I need a strategy to hit that number, that target.

Here is what is very fun with a data-driven strategy, or in this case, an ultra-marathon strategy: I will set an overall strategy and then have sub-strategies to utilize throughout my training to ensure I hit the overarching goal and strategy. In this case, my strategy may be "To finish the Speedgoat 50k in under seven hours by utilizing a strong training schedule of four to five runs per week, partnered with smart cross-training and nutrition." My strategy would be something to this extent for my race and ability to finish it in the time I want. Notice how my strategy statement, which we will cover later in the chapter, includes the desired "outcome" I am looking for. From here, I then set small sub-strategies in place to succeed and ensure the action is put forward. It will be the same for you in your work to become data driven. You will set your outcome. Then, your strategy for achieving that outcome. Finally, you have to put actionable work into place. Just like in an ultra-marathon, I cannot just have a desired outcome and strategy; there must be action in place to make it happen. That is what will be our GAR acronym: Goal to Action to Recycle.

Key pillars

To help us build our data-driven strategy, let's bring in the key pillars that will need to be in place for success. Note: they will be designed differently than for the outcomes. Now that we know our organization's desired data-driven outcome, we need to be able to utilize the pillars in an evolving and strong manner. Those pillars are:

- *Team personnel and structure.* Your strategy needs to include who you will hire to lead the data team, the overall hiring practices for data employees, etc.

- *The "what" and "why."* Your strategy needs to spell out the outcome of your data and why you are doing it.

- *Data management and data integration.* Your strategy needs to include how you will manage and source your data (think of the Cloud), how you will deal with your one or multiple sources of data, etc.

- *"Fail fast" and iteration.* This may seem odd, but your organization needs the ability and culture to truly adopt a fail and learn mentality. I emphasize that this cannot just be talked about but needs to be a part of your data-driven strategy.

- *Analytics processes and methodologies.* Your strategy needs to include thoughts and ideas around the four levels of analytics and how they will be utilized in the organization.

- *Data literacy.* Your strategy needs to include a data literacy strategy and program. We have spoken much on this, so won't belabor the point in this chapter, but more reemphasize the steps and what to do.

- *Data science, machine learning, and artificial intelligence.* Your strategy needs to include how your organization will use and handle the advanced work being done in data and analytics. We know this to be the technical aspect of your data-driven organization, so it can't be done haphazardly.

- *Tools and technology.* Your strategy needs to map out the tools and technologies you will utilize for your data-driven work. It needs to not only tell us what tools and technologies you will have, but also how you plan to deploy and upskill the workforce to utilize them.

- *Data ethics and governance.* Your strategy needs to include your organization's rules and thoughts around the ethical use and governance of your data.
- *Culture.* Your strategy needs to include work around your organization's culture.
- *Data-driven decision making.* Your strategy needs to include a methodology or process for individuals and the organization to adopt and utilize a data-driven decision-making framework.
- *Communication.* Your strategy needs to include how you will disseminate information and the strategy throughout the organization.

These pillars should be considered a part of your overall data strategy. This may seem like a long list, but in fact, when you think about your overall data strategy, the list falls into place. When you know what your outcome is and you build a strategy to get you to that outcome, your overall pillars can fall better into place because you have a direction you are moving in. Let's jump into each pillar to bring it to life for you.

Team personnel and structure

We have spoken throughout this book about different roles within the organization; now let's look at how these roles and positions can be a part of your data strategy. First, let's discuss the positions themselves, and when you find your organization does not have one of these positions or you aren't sure, take the time to audit what you have and then put plans in place to implement change. The roles your data strategy needs to have in place are the following:

- *Chief data (or analytics) officer:* the principal owner of the data strategy. This role owns the data strategy itself, its implementation, and is accountable for its success. The CDO is responsible for the data management, data tools and technologies, data literacy, data ethics, and so forth. In the strategy, write out the roles and responsibilities this person will take on.

- *Executive leadership*: the owners and voices of the data strategy. In the strategy, ensure the responsibility of ownership and evangelizing the data strategy is spelled out for the executive team. Also, ensure in your strategy it is written out that the executive leadership team is also participating in the program, in data literacy, etc. The executive team historically may have been able to know the data work was happening, but throwing it over the wall may have been a norm: out of sight, out of mind. Not anymore. Make it clear and concise that your executive team is a part of this and not just recipients of the data and analytics results.

- *Human resources and learning and development*: when it comes to the data literacy portion of a data strategy, usually the human resources and/or learning and development teams within the organization have responsibility for the data literacy implementation. Build into your strategy the ownership and program of data literacy, which will be spelled out in a later section on how to build this into your strategy.

- *Data science*: notice I did not spell out "data scientist," which would denote the specific role. Instead, I spelled out "data science." There need to be roles that support the data science aspect of your data strategy. In this case, these roles will be more specific towards the latter two levels of analytics: predictive and prescriptive. Ensure you have directed outcomes for these roles. Remember the financial services organization I have mentioned at least once in the book, which hired data scientists into every business unit in the organization but was not finding success with them. Spell out what the data science team is going to be doing. With the holistic strategy and a CDO leading the charge, you may find it much easier for your data scientists to produce value for your organization.

- *Data engineering*: again, here we do not have one title but the world of data engineering in your organization. "Data engineering is the practice of designing and building systems for collecting, storing, and analyzing data at scale" (Coursera, 2021). Data engineering is the field that will make your organization's data and analytical goals possible. The work of a data scientist, data analyst, and end user will be made easier if your data strategy has the pieces in place and spelled out for their work.

- *Data analysts*: the data analysts will make up a large chunk of your professional workforce. Other titles can be business analyst, marketing analyst, etc. The data analyst's work should be focused more around the first two levels of analytics: descriptive and diagnostic. Later in this chapter we will learn about the tools and technologies section of your data strategy. For the data analyst, the tools and technologies matter a lot with regards to what the organization will do with the analysts. A primary responsibility for data analysts is building, using, and maintaining dashboards and visualizations. Ensure the strategy spells out how this will be done.

- *End or business users*: this group will make up the largest consumers and users of your data; it is the rest of the workforce outside of those with "data" and/or "analyst" in their titles. This group is primarily going to be working with descriptive and diagnostic analytics. The democratization of data may be intimidating for this group, as it is not their background, but it is necessary for proper data and analytical success. As a part of the end user portion of the personnel, ensure data literacy is built into the roles' positions in the strategy.

Along with the understanding of the roles and the workforce, the data strategy should work with the human resources and people teams to ensure hiring practices are sound for creating a strong, data-literate workforce. I was asked once if an organization should make data literacy a requirement for hiring new employees. Of course I am going to answer yes, as I am the data literacy guy. The reality is, though, the answer *should* be yes. We look at fundamental skills, like using a computer, as a given for hiring an employee. I think data literacy can be the same here. Ensure your new hires are positioned well to enter your workforce with the right skills, ready to ensure your strategy is in place.

Having the right personnel and structure can be key to your success. The saying goes, if you are prepared, you shall not fear. In this case, having the right people in place can be key to your success. Ensure your data strategy maps out the personnel and roles and responsibilities of each. With this, your organizational workforce structure can be mapped out for data-driven success.

The "what" and "why"

The last chapter was devoted to determining your "what." Now that you have your what, spell it out in your data-driven strategy. Ensure you place the "what" in a clear spot not only in your strategy but around your organization. I want your workforce and culture to be such that the "what" is just a part of everyday living and the "why" could be recited by anyone you ask. If they can't answer it, maybe have them do 10 push-ups. OK we cannot do that. I won't belabor the point here on the "what" and the "why," I think we have covered that enough in the last chapter and throughout the book, but you need to ensure that your data-driven strategy spells it out and it becomes common knowledge in your workforce. Just as readily as your workforce may be able to sing or dance the latest TikTok dance, ensure they can dance the dance of your data outcomes.

Data management and data integration

It goes without saying that within your data-driven strategy there needs to be a section on data management and data integration. In this chapter, we won't speak heavily on the tools and technologies of this area—the next chapter is for that—but we will speak on the principles of data management and data integration. First, let's separate the two of them out and define each of them.

DATA MANAGEMENT
Data management is:

> the practice of collecting, keeping, and using data securely, efficiently, and cost-effectively. The goal of data management is to help people, organizations, and connected things optimize the use of data within the bounds of policy and regulation so that they can make decisions and take actions that maximize the benefit to the organization. (Oracle, 2021)

Think of data management as your organization's ability to manage the total amount of data incoming to the organization and to source, cleanse, and use it effectively. Simple enough, right? If it was simple enough, there wouldn't be so many different articles and books on the topic.

DATA INTEGRATION
Data integration can be understood as a process of combining data from various sources into one place. Beginning with ingestion, it also includes cleaning the data, ETL mapping, and transformation to enable analytics tools to create useful business intelligence (Talend, 2021). Talend also note that there isn't a single, universal approach to data integration, though there are common elements such as networks of data sources and a master server, from which clients access data.

Think of data integration as a piece, an integral piece, of the data management portion of your data-driven strategy.

For your data-driven strategy to work, value needs to be brought to your data. Data is just data and just sits there without an effective data management and data integration story and strategy. Data management is how your organization will optimize the storing of data and bringing it to the forefront of your workforce. Data integration is the process of how your organization will bring that together.

I love the concepts of data management and data integration. I think of these two processes in the world of my ultra-marathon running. The data management would be my training workload and how I am going to manage it all together. Data integration is how I will bring that workload to life and manifest it into my schedule, combining the different types of training I want to do, like running, spinning, lifting, yoga, stretching, and any other types of training I may do. "Data management" is the managing of all the types of training I will do. "Data integration" is how I work those together for maximum benefit.

"Fail fast" and iteration

This might seem like a weird statement or section to put into a data strategy, but this must be the way of thinking and cultural norm in your organization. I hear over and over the old business adage of fail fast and fail often. It is my experience, though, that a lot of organizations talk about failing fast but fail to truly embrace failure. Now, let's make sure we understand that we are not talking about just going out and failing over and over again. The world of data and analytics has a different way of looking at failure.

Statistics, data, and analytics can be seen as a world of probabilities: "If we do 'X,' there is an 80 percent likelihood of 'Y' occurring." This seems pretty straightforward. There is a high likelihood of something happening, 80 percent, but this also means that 20 percent of the time, or one out of five times doing this, it will not occur. So, failure is not necessarily a bad thing in this case. Failure means we hit that one out of five, so the event or process or operation did not go the way we wanted. That is absolutely ok within the world of data and analytics. That is actually something that happens. Whether something has a 1 percent or 99 percent chance of happening, there is still a chance it happens and there is still a chance that something will fall outside of the normal window of the predictability we are looking for. Remember, predictions have modes of failures within them. That is ok.

In the world of data and analytics, we have to establish in our minds—and this is why it is a part of the strategy—this mentality that things will not go the way the data and analytics tell us it will go. This is why we need to fail fast. We aren't looking for fail fast in the traditional sense of just build and fail, build and fail, build and fail. Instead, we are looking to develop the culture and mindset that data and analytics are not perfect, that things, no matter how good an analysis we build, will go in the opposite direction. This is why we have the fail fast and iteration approach.

According to Dictionary.com, iteration can refer to repetition or new versions of something. In your data strategy, build in the language and approach that you will be working in an iterative process. In data and analytics, you will build models, data visualizations, etc., and those will change, evolve, and be modified. Through this process, and it is a process, it should be seen that there is no finish line. As you build these analyses and processes, you will find areas that "fail," that need fine-tuning. Do it. This is your repetition. Data and analytics is a long-haul program, never finishing. For me, like with ultra-marathons, when I finish a race or program, I am on to another. There is no finish, just the next thing. I can iterate, I can improve, find areas and gaps that need fine-tuning. Within your data strategy, do the exact same thing. Find the areas and opportunities to "never finish" and write it out, spell it out.

The mindset of failing and iteration can be key for your organization's culture within data and analytics. A lot of times, people may fear building the analysis or communicating what they have found because of fear of reprisal if the decision based on the analysis doesn't go exactly as hoped or planned. Again, if it doesn't go as planned, that is ok. We take learnings from the analysis and decision, and we iterate on them. By building into your strategy this dialogue and letting people know that if the decision or analysis doesn't go exactly as planned it is ok, then your organization can truly have the culture and data-driven capabilities it needs for success.

Analytics processes and methodologies

Here we are talking about our organization's data-driven strategy and I have a section in that strategy around the analytics processes and methodologies. Why would this section be in this chapter of the book? It is because, remember, analytics is what brings data and information to life. Without analytics, think of data as a sleeping giant that is ready to get to work for you, but is truly just resting. Analytical processes and methodologies are the things that will wake the data giant and put it to work.

Imagine you have a house you need to build, and have the tools, technology, and the materials to build it. You have invested so much money to make it happen, but everything is stagnant and sitting there, nothing happening. You need your workforce to make the house happen. This is analytics. You have your data house materials, technology, and tools just sitting and waiting. Unleash the power of analytics within your organization to bring this house to life. How do you do this? Your data-driven strategy should spell out the analytical tools and techniques you will use.

One example of where this has gone wrong is through the hiring of data scientists. This isn't just with one company I have worked with, but a prevailing theme I have heard over and over again. I have found that many organizations have hired data scientists who are very talented and in a position to drive data success, but they are metaphorically sitting there, doing nothing. In essence, the organization's data house is not being built. Why is this? It is because the cart went before the horse. Organizations are enamored with the idea of data scientists, but clearly do not know how to use them.

THE FOUR LEVELS OF ANALYTICS

As part of the analytical processes and methodologies section of your data strategy, spell out how you want different data roles within the organization to operate, utilizing the four levels of analytics: descriptive, diagnostic, predictive, and prescriptive. To ensure understanding, brief definitions of these four levels can help:

- Descriptive: describes something that has happened or a prediction ahead.
- Diagnostic: is the "why" something happened.
- Predictive: building predictions of what will happen.
- Prescriptive: allowing an external force to drive a decision from the data and analytics.

For the first two levels, spell out how you want descriptive analytics to be utilized throughout the organization. I learned long ago a great way to look at this: make individuals accountable for the data and not just to it. Meaning, don't let your workforce just make a dashboard, being accountable *to* the data, but ensure they use descriptive and diagnostic analytics together, being accountable *for* the data. In your data-driven strategy, ensure the use of and the how-to of descriptive and diagnostic analytics are in place. Ensure these two levels of analytics and their methodologies are designed in a way for the organization to truly gain insight and value from the data to make an insightful decision.

Also make sure it is spelled out how you want to utilize predictive and prescriptive analytics. This is where the data science, data engineering, machine learning, and artificial intelligence come into play. The use of the four levels of analytics is a holistic and iterative model, as we bring that section back in. As an organization, you need to spell out how you will utilize the four levels of analytics and who is responsible for what. Some tips include:

- Everyone is responsible for descriptive analytics. This means the dashboards, KPIs, and reporting of the organization are owned by all. Have your strategy spell out that simplicity is key to the use of descriptive analytics. Along with everyone responsible for these analytics, it should be spelled out that everyone needs to be able to communicate in this realm of analytics.

- Everyone is responsible for diagnostic analytics. Your strategy should spell out techniques and learning around diagnostic analytics, the "why" of analytics. This level should be the most important because it is the golden ticket of data and analytics. Again, everyone should be able to communicate at this level.

- Communication between data roles is key for analytical methodologies. Not everyone needs to know how to do statistics, but everyone needs to communicate effectively within these four levels and between roles in the organization. Herein the world of data fluency comes to life.

- Predictive and prescriptive analytical methodologies are advanced and should be owned by the advanced roles in the organization. Ensure it is stated in your data-driven strategy who owns what work, what tools are used where (more to come on this), and so forth.

These are just a few tips for the use of analytics against data. It may seem silly in one's mind to spell out analytical processes and methodologies in a data-driven strategy, but mapping this portion out can be a recipe for success. I have seen far too many organizations investing in data and tools, but not getting adoption and success. A well-thought-out structure and plan for your analytical work can be key to your data-driven success. You cannot just throw ingredients into a bowl and hope to make the tastiest cookies around. You need a plan, steps, etc., and you need to know how much of each ingredient to add to the recipe. This can be your analytical cookbook recipe.

Think about your favorite cookie you like to eat. Imagine if I told you to add together eggs, flour, sugar, chocolate chips, maybe some vanilla, butter or shortening, etc. Now imagine I don't tell you how much of each to put in. Imagine if there is an order to the recipe and I just buy it all and put it in front of you. Imagine I don't tell you to keep the eggshells out of the recipe. Unfortunately, this is happening in the world of data and analytics today. The ingredients are put in front of people and we are telling them, "go, find us that tasty cookie that will make our business better." Unfortunately, without the recipe spelling things out, the cookies are not tasting the way we want. Trust me, I love cookies and I love data and analytics. With the right recipe, you can make things come to life.

Data literacy

I won't put much more into this section, but it goes without saying that data literacy and learning throughout your organization needs to be a part of your data strategy. I will say that your data literacy needs to be a strategy that complements the desired outcomes of your data. As I met with a large financial institution, as I have shared in this book, and they walked me through their data literacy strategy, I had to ask multiple times if they knew what the organization wanted to do with its data. Unfortunately, they didn't know. All this time and effort was put into a data literacy program, but unfortunately they knew they had to go back and figure out what the organization wanted to do with data. With that, the pair walking me through the strategy could ensure the data literacy strategy tied back through the plans and outcomes for the organization.

Within your data strategy and with a knowledge of the data roles and personalities within your organization, you can ensure the data literacy training is on point for success. Map out the learning paths, assessments, communication plans, and all the data literacy learning towards the end goal of succeeding in your data-driven organization.

Data science, machine learning, and artificial intelligence

Your data strategy should absolutely encompass how data science, machine learning, and artificial intelligence will be deployed within your organization. We have spoken of how many organizations have been caught up with the idea that you can hire data scientists and then your organization will be rolling with data-driven success. Unfortunately, that is not the case. Have you answered how you will use data science to build predictive analytics? Have you answered how you will use machine learning and artificial intelligence for both predictive and prescriptive analytics? If not, you must have a solid knowledge of these bases in data and analytics.

The deployment of these tools, technologies, and advanced data practices will need to be sure to have data management, data integration, data literacy, and be embodied within data-driven decision making. One key understanding within the world of data science, machine learning, and artificial intelligence is the deploying of these models and ensuring automation can occur (Patruno, 2021). Data science, machine learning, and artificial intelligence models and processes work towards an automated front (with data science having a place for data scientists to not automate but work freely in your data and analytical environment). It can take time, energy, resources, and investment to make sure these models are deployed correctly. You need to ensure in your strategy that there is a proper landscape and framework in place that understands the length of time this will take. It is not an easy button, so ensure that it is communicated and understood throughout the organization that this will take time with the proper systems and energy to make it thrive.

These advanced techniques, technologies, and models are powerful and should be used in your strategy: do not leave them out. But ensure they are done right and with the right strategy and mentality.

Tools and technology

We have spoken about roles, personnel, the culture, and all of those pieces, and the next chapter will be a full cover of tools and technologies. In it, we will break down the different areas of tools and technologies that can make up your organization's data stack. Your data strategy should spell out the coverage, investment, and where the tools will deploy. The strategy will also cover what kind of learning strategy will take place to train the employees on these tools and technologies. Let this suffice for now and the next chapter will dive into the different areas of these technologies and give examples of each.

Data ethics and governance

The world is growing more and more concerned with how data is used, the privacy of personal data, biases within machine learning and artificial intelligence, and more. The world is really good at creating data cynicism rather than helping to develop data skepticism, which is healthy. As part of your organization's data strategy, ensure you spell out how the data will be used, the privacy laws that will be followed (think HIPPA laws in healthcare in the United States or GDPR in Europe), and how to ensure biases and other factors do not influence your data in ways that are adverse to how data should be utilized.

To help us understand how to build these parts of the strategy, let me outline what data ethics is. According to Cote (2021), data ethics includes moral obligations related to gathering, storing and using personally identifiable information. Such ethical practices are of utmost concern to analysts, data scientists, information technology professionals—and indeed anyone who handles data.

Your organization's strategy needs to spell out the rules of how data will be handled, how practices will be implemented, how the data will be protected, how your customers will be protected, etc.

With data ethics comes the other similar area of data governance. By definition, data governance is "the process of managing the availability, usability, integrity and security of the data in enterprise systems, based on internal data standards and policies that also control data usage" (Stedman and Vaughan, 2020). With this definition, you can see how data governance can go hand in hand with data ethics and be a part of the overall strategy within your organization.

With data ethics handling privacy laws and more, data governance covers the usage and accessibility of data throughout the organization. With data ethics combining its power with that of data governance, you can see how an organization is set up to succeed with data and avoid some of the perils that can come from the improper use of data. Have the data ethics and governance portions of your strategy checked by legal and compliance, and ensure you not only have strong internal policies and practices, but that your organization is abiding by the laws and regulations that are set forth by governments around the world. As time goes on, more and more of these regulations can be brought forth, ensuring that you will need a strong iterative approach to these topics within your strategy.

Culture

While we have covered in depth what the culture of a data-driven organization looks like, herein we will just mention quickly that of course your data strategy needs to account for how your data-driven organization will refer to and ensure a data-driven culture. You may refer to Chapter 8 to read more about the culture of a data-driven organization.

Data-driven decision making

What is the end goal of data itself? Why is your organization investing in tools, technologies, learning, culture, etc., with regards to data? The end goal is the empowerment of data through the operations and decisions of your organization. Data should lead an organization to drive better decision making.

My friend and colleague, Kevin Hanegan, has really developed a solid system for making decisions with data. In fact, he has a whole book on it, called *Turning Data into Wisdom: How we can collaborate with data to change ourselves, our organizations, and even the world*. In my work with Kevin, he established a smart and sound six-step framework for making a decision (Hanegan, 2019):

- *Ask*: Do you have a smart, data-driven question to answer?
- *Acquire*: With the right question in place, you are set to acquire the right data and information to help you succeed with your decision.
- *Analyze*: Now you can analyze the data you have acquired, helping you arrive at a decision with the data and question you have.

- *Apply*: Herein we apply our human element to make sure we are combining both the human element and data element. We are not here to eliminate one or the other, but to combine them.

- *Announce*: We have to decide and announce our decision, bringing in the key stakeholders for success.

- *Assess*: It is an iterative process, remember? We need to assess the decision and then we can start the process over as we learn.

This six-step framework is a systematic approach to decision making with data in your organization. Take the time to build out a systematic approach to using data for your decision making. This part of the strategy should ensure that the organization is not looking to get rid of the human element, of gut feel. Instead, the system you put in place should spell out the combination of the human experience and skills with the data element. By creating a framework in your organization to use data in your decision-making processes, you can excel and accelerate the purpose of data: to enhance decision making.

Communication

Now why does a data strategy have a section on communication in it? Why would this matter? The reality is, proper communication is essential for your organization to truly adopt, adapt, and succeed with data. I am fond of asking: How many of us like that email hitting our inbox that says you now have mandatory training? If you are like me, you don't like it and it isn't something you look forward to doing. So, if you do not have strong communication around your data strategy, culture, data-driven decision making, etc., how can you expect your organization to take this on and succeed?

For your communication strategy, ensure there is a three-part system to the communication:

- *Why*: establish and ensure the organization understands the why of your data strategy.

- *What*: spell out what it is you are doing.

- *How*: how your organization will use data, implement the strategy, and so forth.

Along with the strategy around communication, ensure you use some tips and tricks to establish all the key elements of your strategy:

- *Community*: build out a data community in your organization. Many people are not comfortable with data, don't know how to use it, or just don't know where to start, among other things. A community in place can leave an open forum for people to chat and receive help. A data community is where individuals can go to learn, share, and ask questions with regard to data and analytics. Leadership should sign off on this data community, and it should be owned with the data part of an organization. From a functionality perspective, tools like Microsoft Teams are powerful for discussions. These communities can also create events for individuals to attend to learn more and grow.
- *Webinars and thought leadership*: utilize webinars and thought leadership to drive home points, get buy-in, and instruct your organization around topics in data.

Overall, a strong communication plan can go a long way to help create buy-in and success with data. Don't fall prey to old ways of doing things and just think you can roll out a plan. Instead, use communication and transparency to really emphasize your plan.

Conclusion

Wow, that was a lot of information. Herein I covered areas that should be considered essential for your strategy. There are overlaps and some parts are easier than others. Here is that list again:

- *Team personnel and structure*. Your strategy needs to include who you will hire to lead the data team, the overall hiring practices for data employees, etc.

- *The "what" and "why."* Your strategy needs to spell out the outcome of your data and why you are doing it.

- *Data management and data integration.* Your strategy needs to include how you will manage and source your data (think of the Cloud), how you will deal with your one or multiple sources of data, etc.

- *"Fail fast" and iteration.* This may seem odd, but your organization needs the ability and culture to truly adopt a fail and learn mentality. I emphasize that this cannot just be talked about but needs to be a part of your data-driven strategy.

- *Analytics processes and methodologies.* Your strategy needs to include thoughts and ideas around the four levels of analytics and how they will be utilized in the organization.

- *Data literacy.* Your strategy needs to include a data literacy strategy and program.

- *Data science, machine learning, and artificial intelligence.* Your strategy needs to include how your organization will use and handle the advanced work being done in data and analytics. We know this to be the technical aspect of your data-driven organization, so it can't be done haphazardly.

- *Tools and technology.* Your strategy needs to map out the tools and technologies you will utilize for your data-driven work. It needs to not only tell us what tools and technologies you will have, but also how you plan to deploy and upskill the workforce to utilize them.

- *Data ethics and governance.* Your strategy needs to include your organization's rules and thoughts around the ethical use and governance of your data.

- *Culture.* Your strategy needs to include work around your organization's culture.

- *Data-driven decision making.* Your strategy needs to include a methodology or process for individuals and the organization to adopt and utilize a data-driven decision-making framework.

- *Communication.* Your strategy needs to include how you will disseminate information and the strategy throughout the organization.

Work hard to build out your strategy successfully. You have your outcome and now your key pieces for a strategy. In our next chapter we will discuss the tools and technologies that will enable and empower you for success.

11

Be data driven—start your journey!

We have covered a lot in this book; you could write a book on each chapter's topic. The key is getting started and not hesitating and really putting the work in. Through this book, we have covered many topics that will stick out and empower you to build a data-driven organization. In this chapter, we want to do two things: 1) review each chapter and its key points, and 2) get you motivated and excited to tap into your organization's true potential and ability to succeed with data. We have listed so many important points, pillars, and characteristics of a data-driven organization. To end this book, we will bring it around and give a quick set of "Start Your Journey" notes. Overall, your ability to use data can help your organization thrive now and into the future economy. As you work to implement things you learned through this book, remember, it is a process and not a quick fix or easy button that will help you succeed with data. I am excited for you and your journey. Let's jump into the key points of each chapter.

Chapter 1: A data-driven world

In the first chapter, we dove into just how important data is in the world. If you recall, we looked at the evolution of data and mentioned a few things that are accelerating the production and consumption of data today:

- *Smartphones and social media.* These two things, smartphones and social media, represent a treasure trove of data for an organization looking to utilize data, especially with your work with your end consumers.

- *Sensors and the Internet of Things.* The world has a connectivity addiction: everything is becoming connected. These connections and sensors, spanning across many different areas of business and our lives, produce much data. This then can translate into usable data for organizations. Personally, I like some of these sensors and connections that look to improve my life.

- *Smart homes.* Last time I checked, I do not need a smart refrigerator (although I have kids who love to draw pictures on the screen). I do not need a phone that will connect to the water sprinkling system for my lawn. The reality is, though, that smart homes and smart devices, like the phone, are all over the world. By using these devices, the companies that own and produce them are able to understand our habits and work on a micro-level. This can then help them to target us more effectively. Not only that, but some devices can learn and adjust for us.

- *Fitness trackers.* A lot of us are wearing devices that will collect data on our fitness. I am wearing one right now. It connects to my phone and I can track personal data points.

- *Vehicles, grids, and data artifacts.* I think we all are aware of the work in automated cars and the connectivity this brings to our lives.

Overall, this data-driven world is powerful when we harness the power of data, when an organization is truly data driven. This term "data driven" can have multiple meanings. For our purposes, it means an individual, team, or organization is using data to enhance and improve operations and decision making.

Chapter 2: The impact of Covid-19 on organizations and data

It is no secret: Covid-19 impacted our lives in drastic fashion, as it did businesses and data. I watched as my calendar filled with meetings with organizations looking to succeed with data. What I witnessed was that Covid-19 sped up the process for organizations with their data-driven strategies. As organizations *wanted* to be data driven, Covid-19 forced them to not play a waiting game anymore. Covid-19 forced organizations to speed up their data-driven work and strategies.

In this chapter, we listed some trends within industries and organizations:

- Adapting and building the right data-driven culture is crucial to the success of an organization.
- Organizations are investing in upskilling and reskilling initiatives to ensure they can compete in the future economy.
- Investment in data tools and technology is rising, including an increase in movement of data to the Cloud.
- Every region and industry around the world is being pushed to be data driven.
- Data and analytical strategies and the hiring of leaders to lead these data strategies are on the rise.

One key area where Covid-19 opened the eyes of organizations is the need to have the right leadership in place. If organizations have haphazard organizational structures, if workers aren't led by a strong data-driven strategy, then the organization may be failing or not seeing the return on investment it desires. Covid-19 has sped up the data-driven world, regardless of region or industry.

Chapter 3: Technologies advancing data and analytics, and the need for the human element

The world of data and analytics is full of tools and technologies. Sometimes I think too many. We are inundated and have so many choices, so many different opportunities, how does one decide? How can we work through all these technologies to enable success? How does the human element come into play? Through this chapter, we shared different roles within the organization as they pertain to data.

We also mentioned different types of tools your organization may invest in to help in your data-driven strategy. To review, the roles were:

- *Data scientist.* This is the more advanced practitioner, working the more technical aspects of data, such as statistics and machine learning.

- *Data analyst.* This role is more common in an organization and may even take on different names, like business or marketing analyst. This role is not as advanced as a data scientist, but works with data and analytics a part of their job.

- *Data engineer.* This role is all about empowering the end users by "engineering" the data for those users.

- *Business user.* The most common data role in an organization. The business user is not a data professional by title, but is someone who now needs to utilize data in their job. This role is the essence of data literacy.

- *Leadership.* This seems like a unique role for an organization with regard to data. The reality is, leadership is a key role when it comes to data. Leadership has ownership and helps ensure the organization is operating in a data-driven manner. Later in the book, we explored the gaps within leadership.

With an understanding of the data roles within an organization, it becomes easier to understand the tools and technologies available:

- *Business intelligence and data visualization.* These are some of the most common data tools available today. Common ones are Microsoft Excel, Tableau, and Qlik.

- *Data science.* Different tools are enabling the field of data science. These tools will empower data science to work in your organization.

- *Coding languages.* Coding languages are very popular in the data world. Such languages include R and Python.

- *Artificial intelligence.* Artificial intelligence is aiming for machines to work like humans.

- *Machine learning.* The robots are taking over! OK, no, not really. Machine learning is where the machine learns and operates on its own.
- *Cloud.* The Cloud is a powerful way for organizations to store and utilize data.
- *Databases.* A database is a data warehouse, to be used by organizations to store data.
- *Data lake.* An accessible tool and technology that allows an organization to store multiple data sources in one area.
- *Human capital.* The most indispensable data tool and technology in the world. Human capital is an essential element. It is your workforce. The individuals with unique skills and talents to bring data to life.

Chapter 4: What is a data-driven organization?

The title of this book is "Be Data Driven." What does that mean? In this chapter we covered just that. Data driven essentially means utilizing data and analytics to improve your organization and drive decisions—that's it. There is no need for lengthy, flashy definitions.

In the chapter, we covered five pillars of being data driven:

- *Strategy.* What are we doing?
- *Leadership.* Who owns what we are doing?
- *Data literacy.* Do we have the skills to accomplish what we are doing?
- *Data and technology.* Do we have the data, access, and tools for data-driven decision making?
- *Culture.* Is the environment ready to succeed with data?

Overall, there are many aspects that make up a data-driven organization. Most, if not all, of those will fall within the five pillars of a data-driven organization. The key is progressing towards the right journey.

Chapter 5: Foundational skills gaps

Within the world of data and analytics, organizations are not seeing the adoption of data and analytical work. Without this adoption, organizations are not seeing the return on investment they could if the organization closed these gaps. There are different skills gaps within organizations, which in turn prevents them from being data driven.

The first skills gap that organizations are seeing is the fundamental skills gap of data literacy. Data literacy is essentially the ability of an individual to confidently and comfortably use data. It is not that everyone needs to be a data scientist, but everyone needs to develop the fundamental ability to utilize data effectively to make decisions. Data literacy can empower individuals to use the data and analytics the organization provides, and the tools and technologies, more effectively.

Within data literacy, we spoke about the four levels of analytics: descriptive, diagnostic, predictive, and prescriptive. The reality is, not everyone needs to develop talents and abilities to succeed in each area of analytics. Instead, organizations need to utilize the right skills throughout the four levels of analytics. The first two levels more fundamentally deal with data literacy, whereas the second two levels are more technical and advanced.

With this fundamental gap, we defined an approach for an organization become more data literate:

- *Assess your workforce.* What skills and gaps exist?
- *Communication plans.* Are you communicating why you are working to be data driven?
- *Persona- or role-based learning programs.* Create learning paths and programs based on the data roles in the organization.
- *Cohort approach to learning.* Bucket learners in cohorts to help with effective learning.
- *Metrics and measurement.* Measure and understand the impact of your data literacy program.
- *Iterative approach.* Data and analytics needs to be based on a learn and iterate approach.

Chapter 6: Pillars of an organizational data strategy

Not only are there gaps and holes within an organization's data literacy and its workforce, the data-driven strategies in the world leave a lot wanting. In this chapter we found the key pillars that have gaps that need to be solved. In Chapter 10, of course, we build your data strategy for you (at least help lay your foundation). The pillars in Chapter 6 are:

- *Outcome.* What do you want to achieve and are we tying our data back to our organization's business strategy?
- *Culture.* Is our organization ready to handle being data driven? (This is the most key element of being data driven.)
- *Data storage.* Are we using the right strategy to build the backend of our data philosophy and strategy?
- *Analytics.* Do we have proper use of the four levels of analytics within our organization?
- *Leadership.* Do we have the right structure and people in place to lead a data-driven strategy and do they have the right skills?
- *Tools and technology.* Do we have the right tools in place to enable our organization to succeed in a data-driven position?
- *Data literacy.* Do we have the right skill sets throughout the organization and if not, do we have the right upskilling, reskilling, and learning programs in place to ensure our data strategy is implemented properly?
- *Communication.* Do we have the proper communication in place to transmit information and data throughout the organization effectively?
- *Ethics.* Do we have the right ethical use of data in place to help us as an organization use data effectively and in the right manner?

For organizations to succeed with data, these gaps need to be addressed. In Chapter 10, the number of pillars exceeds those in this chapter and that is intentional. If you build your strategy correctly, you should see the gaps disappear in your organization's data strategy.

Chapter 7: The gap in leadership

Unfortunately, there is a large skills gap within leadership in organizations around the world. It is imperative for an organization's leadership to be data literate and understand how to build a data-driven organization. In this chapter, we covered key areas within executive leadership that need to be addressed for an organization to be data driven. Those areas are:

- *Data literacy*. Executive leaders must have data literacy confidence, with a mindset for continuous learning.
- *Digital literacy*. Executive leaders must have a sound understanding of technology and its empowerment (think the Cloud).
- *Change management*. Leadership needs to have a sound understanding of change management principles to adapt and evolve with data and analytics.
- *Strategic thinking*. Do leaders truly know how to strategically think through data and analytical strategies? What they want to do with data?
- *Chief data officer*. Does your organization have the right leadership in place for data and analytical success?
- *Communication*. One key with data and analytics is transparent, effective communication.

Along with looking at executive leadership in an organization, we addressed the other leadership that will be tasked with leading and implementing the sections of the data-driven strategy; we called this the "tiered leadership." The areas of focus for tiered leadership were:

- a sound understanding of the data strategy
- the open and honest use of data
- a strong data literacy skill set

Overall, leadership is vital to the success of a data-driven organization. With strong leadership setting the example, the organization can follow.

Chapter 8: The biggest hurdle: culture

It is no secret that culture is the biggest hurdle for a data-driven organization. It isn't the tools, data cleanliness, etc.—it is the culture. In this chapter we learned the key characteristics that make up a data-driven culture. Those are:

- *Data fluency*. Does your organization speak the language of data?
- *Adaptability*. Are your employees well armed and trained to deal with change, including the shift and evolution of their roles?
- *Continuous learning*. We know about learning, but are your employees in a sound position to succeed with continuous learning?
- *Diversified skill sets*. Are you hiring employees with diverse backgrounds or are you only looking for the same advanced, technical skills like data science?
- *Growth vs fixed mindset*. Are they armed with a growth mindset?
- *Gamification and reward-based systems*. Do you have a good system in place to reward your employees within your data-driven organization?
- *Embracing failure*. You may say the adage "fail fast," but do you truly adopt it?
- *Clear vision and strategy*. Do your employees know and embrace your data strategy?
- *Grassroots*. Does your organization employ both a top-down AND a bottom-up approach?
- *Recognition of biases*. Does your organization recognize and understand its biases within?

Chapter 9: Decide your outcome

In Chapter 9, we informed you that the way to start is to decide your outcome. The pillars of deciding your outcome are:

- *Get the right people involved*. Do you have the right personnel in place to set the outcome? Do they have the right skills?

- *Hold planning meetings.* Set in place planning meetings. Note: these should not be all-day meetings, where you are locked in a room for eight hours straight, working through lunch. We spoke about the effectiveness of meetings and setting the right tone.

- *Understand your current situation.* Do you know your current data-driven situation? Do you have the landscape in place? What are the skills of the organization? What tools and technologies do you have?

- *Establish the "why."* Do you know your "why" behind doing these things? Are you just doing something because you read about it online, heard about it from a peer or colleague, or are you doing it just because you think it should be done? Know your why!

- *Know your business strategy inside and out.* Do you have a good grasp of what the business is trying to do? If you are a leader, do you know what you truly want to accomplish as a business? If you are an employee, do you understand what your business is doing and your role in it? Hint: a lot of employees may not truly know this, so it is very important.

- *Do not boil the ocean.* Are you trying to take on too much within the business and data? If you are not a very data-driven company right now, can you start off by setting small outcomes and creating a library of wins? Hint: this can be a great way to set the tone for your business.

- *Set your outcome statement and vision.* Do you have an outcome statement and vision that is set and then shared throughout the organization? Is this top of people's minds as they work with data? Have you had each business unit and area set out smaller outcome statements that roll up into the overall outcome statement?

Chapter 10: Build your strategy

In our last chapter, we gave you ways to build your data-driven strategy. Having the right strategy can empower you to succeed towards your outcome. To set your strategy, the keys were:

- *Team personnel and structure.* Your strategy needs to include who you will hire to lead the data team, the overall hiring practices for data employees, etc.

- *The "what" and "why."* Your strategy needs to spell out the outcome of your data and why you are doing it.

- *Data management and data integration.* Your strategy needs to include how you will manage and source your data (think of the Cloud), how you will deal with your one or multiple sources of data, etc.

- *"Fail fast" and iteration.* This may seem odd, but your organization needs the ability and culture to truly adopt a fail and learn mentality. I emphasize that this cannot just be talked about but needs to be a part of your data-driven strategy.

- *Analytics processes and methodologies.* Your strategy needs to include thoughts and ideas around the four levels of analytics and how they will be utilized in the organization.

- *Data literacy.* Your strategy needs to include a data literacy strategy and program.

- *Data science, machine learning, and artificial intelligence.* Your strategy needs to include how your organization will use and handle the advanced work being done in data and analytics. We know this to be the technical aspect of your data-driven organization, so it can't be done haphazardly.

- *Tools and technology.* Your strategy needs to map out the tools and technologies you will utilize for your data-driven work. It needs to not only tell us what tools and technologies you will have, but also how you plan to deploy and upskill the workforce to utilize them.

- *Data ethics and governance.* Your strategy needs to include your organization's rules and thoughts around the ethical use and governance of your data.

- *Culture.* Your strategy needs to include work around your organization's culture.

- *Data-driven decision making.* Your strategy needs to include a methodology or process for individuals and the organization to adopt and utilize a data-driven decision-making framework.

- *Communication.* Your strategy needs to include how you will disseminate information and the strategy throughout the organization.

Conclusion

Now that we have reviewed each chapter, let me turn us back to my world of ultra-marathon running. Ultra-marathons are a different kind of beast for racing. The terrain, the weather, the conditions, your fuel and running strategy, so many things affect and are a part of your race. For an ultra-marathon, you have advice and steps you can take to help you have a good race, giving you the best chance to finish. These steps can be utilized within a data-driven organization, too.

- *Step 1: Race intentionally.* Each and every ultra-marathon is your own race. If you try to run someone else's race, you can fail very easily. Each individual in the race is different, with different skills and abilities. If you don't maintain your race for yourself, you can push yourself too hard. This can spell disaster for an ultra-marathon. The same can be true within a data-driven organization. As you build your organization, don't try to "keep up with the Joneses." Run your own race. Don't buy the latest tool because your competitor did—it may not work for you. Instead, be intentional in how you build your data-driven organization.

- *Step 2: Race intelligently.* One time I heard an ultra-runner say, "start slow, and then go slower." This means, don't go out too fast; I use that saying now. I am also fond of saying you can't win a race in the first few miles, but you can certainly lose it. Meaning, if you go out too hard, you can burn out early in the race, causing you lots of pain and trouble. If you start slower, you can preserve your reserves for later in the race. Throughout the race, choose the right pace, feel out where your condition is, and so forth. The same can be said in a data-driven organization. Don't boil the ocean. You can't do everything overnight. Instead, start smart and intelligently, and as you build and grow, work through your process to truly become more and more data driven.

- *Step 3: Push the pace.* Now, ultra-marathons are long. Usually seen as the starting distance, you are tasked at a 50k or around 31 miles. That is a big race, not to mention that you are on trails and mountains, going up and down. You may even deal with elevation above sea level, like my race in Leadville, Colorado, where the town sits over 10,000 feet above sea level. All that said, you need to push the pace. Races can have cutoffs and those may be aggressive. If you just work through, maybe sit lazy for a bit, it can come back to bite you later on in the race. Within a data-driven organization, you need to be intentional and intelligent within your organization's data-driven work, but you need to push the pace. The reality is, the data world is not getting any younger. On the contrary, we are seeing advancements all the time within data and analytics. We need to push the pace to ensure our organization doesn't get left behind.

- *Step 4: Fuel correctly.* In an ultra-marathon, you are burning a lot of calories over a race. In a 50k, I may burn 5,000 or more calories. I usually have a strategy to eat fuel every hour during a race. Then, when I am at an aid station, I will eat more. Plus, I need to keep hydrated throughout the race. Proper fuel and hydration can be in place to help you not "bonk" in a race. In data and analytics, you must be fueling on a regular basis. You must be learning about the new tools and technologies, and advancing your skills in data literacy. You must be adapting and adopting analytical methodologies. The world of data and analytics is evolving, and your organization must evolve with it. At times, "bonks" can occur that an organization wasn't planning—think Covid-19. As you fuel correctly, hopefully you can evolve, develop, and succeed within a data-driven organization, helping you to withstand the drastic shifts in front of you.

- *Step 5: Smile throughout.* Ultra-marathons are painful. During races, you have moments of agony, pain, but also joy and jubilation. Your attitude can determine so much during your race. With the right frame of mind, you can be more successful within your ultra-marathon. As you go through a journey to be data driven, you are going to experience pain, agony, external forces, moments of joy, and moments of success. Choose to enjoy the journey as you go through it.

Thank you for taking this journey through this book. Data and analytics presents such a powerful moment and opportunity for individuals and organizations. It is our time to seize our journeys. Don't hesitate—start your journey today!

REFERENCES

Chapter 1

Business Wire (2021) Global spending on big data and analytics solutions will reach $215.7 billion in 2021, according to a new IDC spending guide, https://www.businesswire.com/news/home/20210817005182/en/ (archived at https://perma.cc/8NTY-VQVB)

Forbes Insights (2019) Rethinking the role of chief data officer, https://www.forbes.com/sites/insights-intelai/2019/05/22/rethinking-the-role-of-chief-data-officer/?sh=4c72de351bf9 (archived at https://perma.cc/S5CT-567A)

Merriam-Webster Dictionary (2021) Data, https://www.merriam-webster.com/dictionary/data (archived at https://perma.cc/9P6X-XH4S)

Mingis, K and Montgomery, A (2021) The evolution of Apple's iPhone, *Computer World*, https://www.computerworld.com/article/2604020/the-evolution-of-apples-iphone.html (archived at https://perma.cc/RJ6T-FAQ3)

Morrow, J (2021) *Be Data Literate: The data literacy skills everyone needs to succeed*, Kogan Page, London

Oracle (2021) What is IoT? https://www.oracle.com/internet-of-things/what-is-iot/ (archived at https://perma.cc/MWF9-A7U3)

ProductPlan (2021) Technical Debt, https://www.productplan.com/glossary/technical-debt/ (archived at https://perma.cc/KE88-GEYW)

Propane (2018) The Internet of Things: How businesses can increase revenue in digital commerce, https://propane.agency/lux/the-internet-of-things-how-businesses-can-increase-revenue-in-digital-commerce/ (archived at https://perma.cc/T8RV-GZTS)

Qlik (2020) New research from Accenture and Qlik shows the data skills gap is costing organizations billions in lost productivity, https://www.qlik.com/us/company/press-room/press-releases/data-skills-gap-is-costing-organizations-billions-in-lost-productivity (archived at https://perma.cc/EW92-JW2Q)

Rack Solutions Blog (2018) New prediction from IDC says worldwide data to reach 175 zettabytes by 2025, https://www.racksolutions.com/news/blog/new-prediction-from-idc-says-worldwide-data-to-reach-175-zettabytes-by-2025/ (archived at https://perma.cc/NN8W-FRSL)

Saha, D (2020) How the world became data-driven, and what's next, *Forbes*, https://www.forbes.com/sites/googlecloud/2020/05/20/how-the-world-became-data-driven-and-whats-next/?sh=10392e8257fc (archived at https://perma.cc/UL3Q-FVVQ)

The Great Hack (2019) https://www.thegreathack.com (archived at https://perma.cc/CYD2-9G2V)

Chapter 2

Cambridge Dictionary (2021) https://dictionary.cambridge.org/us/dictionary/english/reskilling (archived at https://perma.cc/D8Q8-SPT9)

Harapko, S (2021) How COVID-19 impacted supply chains and what comes next, *EY*, https://www.ey.com/en_us/supply-chain/how-covid-19-impacted-supply-chains-and-what-comes-next (archived at https://perma.cc/5UTS-6FAP)

Jeans, D (2021) Companies Will Spend $50 Billion on Artificial Intelligence This Year With Little To Show For It, *Forbes*, www.forbes.com/sites/davidjeans/2020/10/20/bcg-mit-report-shows-companies-will-spend-50-billion-on-artificial-intelligence-with-few-results/?sh=6217833f7c87 (archived at https://perma.cc/UM9S-5S9W)

Leybzon, D (2020) Bad data visualizations in the time of COVID-19, *Medium*, https://medium.com/nightingale/bad-data-visualization-in-the-time-of-covid-19-5a9f8198ce3e (archived at https://perma.cc/BC27-XBM8)

Merriam-Webster (2021) Upskill, https://www.merriam-webster.com/dictionary/upskill (archived at https://perma.cc/E66H-NH9E)

Petrov, C (2021) 25 impressive big data statistics for 2021, *Techjury*, https://techjury.net/blog/big-data-statistics/#gref (archived at https://perma.cc/7N99-729R)

Tableau (2021) Data Culture, https://www.tableau.com/why-tableau/data-culture (archived at https://perma.cc/WZ9H-TWQ6)

Chapter 3

AWS Amazon (2021) What is a data lake? https://aws.amazon.com/big-data/datalakes-and-analytics/what-is-a-data-lake/ (archived at https://perma.cc/FA4E-ZJQU)

Cal University of Pennsylvania (2021) Data science: One of the fastest growing occupations, https://www.calu.edu/academics/undergraduate/bachelors/data-science/jobs-career-salaries.aspx (archived at https://perma.cc/A3M4-RKHT)

Cha, B (2015) Too embarrassed to ask: what is "the cloud" and how does it work? *VOX*, https://www.vox.com/2015/4/30/11562024/too-embarrassed-to-ask-what-is-the-cloud-and-how-does-it-work (archived at https://perma.cc/3ADX-FJRE)

Coursera (2021) What is a data engineer? A guide to this in-demand career, https://www.coursera.org/articles/what-does-a-data-engineer-do-and-how-do-i-become-one (archived at https://perma.cc/MZL3-CCWA)

DataRobot (2021) Data Science, https://www.datarobot.com/wiki/data-science/ (archived at https://perma.cc/8BR4-XM3U)

eWeek Editors (2020) Why enterprises struggle with cloud data lakes, *eWeek*, https://www.eweek.com/storage/why-enterprises-struggle-with-cloud-data-lakes/ (archived at https://perma.cc/U4AV-4TRQ)

Forbes Technology Council (2020) 12 top recommended database management tools, *Forbes,* https://www.forbes.com/sites/forbestechcouncil/2020/01/08/12-top-recommended-database-management-tools/?sh=5d4fcc433cd3 (archived at https://perma.cc/NH9D-ZHPF)

Fridman, L (2019) Deep learning basics: Introduction and overview, *YouTube*, https://www.youtube.com/watch?v=O5xeyoRL95U (archived at https://perma.cc/TLW3-DPZH)

Fruhlinger, J and Pratt, M (2019) What is business intelligence? Transforming data into insights, *CIO.com*, https://www.cio.com/article/2439504/business-intelligence-definition-and-solutions.html (archived at https://perma.cc/3R5V-GZ24)

IBM Cloud Education (2020a) Artificial Intelligence (AI), https://www.ibm.com/cloud/learn/what-is-artificial-intelligence (archived at https://perma.cc/H5UM-UNSB)

IBM Cloud Education (2020b) Machine learning, https://www.ibm.com/cloud/learn/machine-learning (archived at https://perma.cc/44XV-F2PW)

Jeans, D (2020) Companies will spend $50 billion on artificial intelligence this year with little to show for it, *Forbes*, https://www.forbes.com/sites/davidjeans/2020/10/20/bcg-mit-report-shows-companies-will-spend-50-billion-on-artificial-intelligence-with-few-results/?sh=4934120c7c87 (archived at https://perma.cc/A4KN-XPDZ)

Oracle (2021) What is a database? https://www.oracle.com/database/what-is-database/ (archived at https://perma.cc/7EHK-2L2Z)

Rosenbaum, E (2019) Tech spending will near $4 trillion this year. Here's where all the money is going and why, *CNBC*, https://www.cnbc.com/2019/04/08/4-trillion-in-tech-spending-in-2019-heres-where-the-money-is-going.html (archived at https://perma.cc/JXC5-MMCJ)

Tableau (2021) What is data visualization? Definition, examples, and learning resources, https://www.tableau.com/learn/articles/data-visualization (archived at https://perma.cc/6WQS-3MZA)

Chapter 4

At Internet (2021) Data-driven, https://www.atinternet.com/en/glossary/data-driven (archived at https://perma.cc/8ZJ6-9TVX)

Kopanakis, J (2021) 5 real-world examples of how brands are using big data analytics, *Mentionlytics*, https://www.mentionlytics.com/blog/5-real-world-examples-of-how-brands-are-using-big-data-analytics/ (archived at https://perma.cc/PLE8-6TJT)

Management Study Guide (2021) Strategy – definition and features, https://www.managementstudyguide.com/strategy-definition.htm (archived at https://perma.cc/4X9W-F2D2)

Petrov, C (2021) 25+ impressive big data statistics for 2021, *Techjury*, https://techjury.net/blog/big-data-statistics/#gref (archived at https://perma.cc/7N99-729R)

Price, A (2021) 5 secrets to Airbnb's marketing success, *Annex Cloud*, https://www.annexcloud.com/blog/5-secrets-to-airbnbs-marketing-success/ (archived at https://perma.cc/Q3ZE-R6Q4)

Qlik (2021) What is data literacy? https://www.qlik.com/us/bi/data-literacy (archived at https://perma.cc/9DT3-KUCW)

Schroer, A, (2019) From fighting cancer to preventing disease, big data in healthcare might just save your life, *Built In*, https://builtin.com/big-data/big-data-in-healthcare (archived at https://perma.cc/MK3A-778L)

Selinger, D (2014) Data driven: What Amazon's Jeff Bezos taught me about running a company, *Entrepreneur*, https://www.entrepreneur.com/article/237326 (archived at https://perma.cc/ZAL6-2FQZ)

Sykes, N (2018) 5 companies using Big Data and AI to improve performance, *Kolabtree Blog*, https://www.kolabtree.com/blog/5-companies-using-big-data-and-ai-to-improve-performance/ (archived at https://perma.cc/RV4G-NVNX)

Visiongain Ltd (2021) Big data analytics in healthcare market worth US \$101 billion by 2031: Visiongain Research Inc, *Globe Newswire*, https://www.globenewswire.com/news-release/2021/06/23/2252041/0/en/Big-Data-Analytics-in-Healthcare-Market-worth-US-101-Billion-by-2031-Visiongain-Research-Inc.html (archived at https://perma.cc/2RBT-QEZJ)

Chapter 5

Goodreads.com (2021) Nelson Mandela quotes, https://www.goodreads. com/quotes/9041891-i-never-lose-i-either-win-or-learn   (archived   at https://perma.cc/XU7S-XW7B)

Impact (2021) The state of data analytics adoption, https://www.impactmy biz.com/blog/data-analytics-adoption-what-it-means/   (archived   at https://perma.cc/QR8A-JBVR)

Levesque, EM (2019) Understanding the skills gap – and what employers can do about it, *Brookings*, https://www.brookings.edu/research/under standing-the-skills-gap-and-what-employers-can-do-about-it/   (archived at https://perma.cc/W83L-DCHC)

Mackenzie, G (2021) If you can't measure it, you can't improve it, *Guava Box*, https://guavabox.com/if-you-cant-measure-it-you-cant-improve-it/ (archived at https://perma.cc/FGU5-QB98)

Panetta, K (2021) A data and analytics leader's guide to data literacy, *Gartner*, https://www.gartner.com/smarterwithgartner/a-data-and-analytics-leaders-guide-to-data-literacy (archived at https://perma.cc/ W6JH-GQCW)

Qlik (2021) What is data literacy? https://www.qlik.com/us/bi/data-literacy (archived at https://perma.cc/9DT3-KUCW)

The Data Literacy Project (2021) The Data Literacy Index, https://thedata literacyproject.org/resources (archived at https://perma.cc/FW23-63B3)

Your Dictionary (2021) Cohort, https://www.yourdictionary.com/cohort (archived at https://perma.cc/R3QQ-RR3P)

Chapter 6

Lotame (2019) How to build a data strategy, https://www.lotame.com/how-to-build-a-data-strategy/ (archived at https://perma.cc/Y7QF-PY4T)

Marr, B (2021) Why every business needs a data and analytics strategy, *Bernard Marr & Co*, https://bernardmarr.com/why-every-business-needs-a-data-and-analytics-strategy/ (archived at https://perma.cc/DP66-85ZC)

Janiszewska-Kiewra, E Podlesny J, and Soller H (2021) Ethical data usage in an era of digital technology and regulation, McKinsey Digital, https://www. mckinsey.com/business-functions/mckinsey-digital/our-insights/tech-forward/ethical-data-usage-in-an-era-of-digital-technology-and-regulation (archived at https://perma.cc/9JMF-HCEW)

Merriam-Webster   (2021)   Strategy,   https://www.merriam-webster.com/ dictionary/strategy (archived at https://perma.cc/B9PM-3S6F)

Chapter 7

Aguirre, D and Alpern, M (2014) 10 principles of leading change management, *Strategy+Business*, https://www.strategy-business.com/article/00255 (archived at https://perma.cc/ZY5A-H4WZ)

Center for Creative Leadership (2020) The leadership gap: How to fix what your organization lacks, https://www.ccl.org/articles/leading-effectively-articles/leadership-gap-what-you-still-need/ (archived at https://perma.cc/8JQR-UR7U)

Effective Governance (2021) What is "strategic thinking"? https://www.effectivegovernance.com.au/page/knowledge-centre/news-articles/what-is-strategic-thinking (archived at https://perma.cc/553P-EFXJ)

Forbes Insights (2019) Rethinking the role of chief data officer, *Forbes*, https://www.forbes.com/sites/insights-intelai/2019/05/22/rethinking-the-role-of-chief-data-officer/?sh=4b074b11bf9b (archived at https://perma.cc/F6WN-AFPJ)

Merriam-Webster (2021) Leadership, https://www.merriam-webster.com/dictionary/leadership (archived at https://perma.cc/W2DK-MY6J)

Morrell, J (2021) The role of chief data officers (CDOs) in 2021, *Datameer*, https://www.datameer.com/blog/the-role-of-chief-data-officers-in-2021/ (archived at https://perma.cc/KY6N-4C9A)

Neal, S (2021) What a leadership skills gap analysis of 15,000 leaders reveals about the future, *DDI*, https://www.ddiworld.com/blog/leadership-skills-gap (archived at https://perma.cc/L6GE-V5U2)

Olavsrud, T and Zetlin, M (2020) What is a chief data officer? A leader who creates business value from data, *CIO.com*, https://www.cio.com/article/3234884/what-is-a-chief-data-officer.html (archived at https://perma.cc/UER2-E9DP)

Prosci (2021) Thought leadership articles. Definition of change management, https://www.prosci.com/resources/articles/definition-of-change-management (archived at https://perma.cc/ESL9-DJ6G)

Qlik (2021) What is data literacy? https://www.qlik.com/us/bi/data-literacy (archived at https://perma.cc/9DT3-KUCW)

Renaissance (2021) What is digital literacy and why does it matter? https://www.renaissance.com/2019/02/08/blog-digital-literacy-why-does-it-matter/ (archived at https://perma.cc/UXG7-Y75H)

Stedman, C and Vaughan, J (2020) What is data governance and why does it matter? *TechTarget*, https://searchdatamanagement.techtarget.com/definition/data-governance (archived at https://perma.cc/CNA8-L5UH)

The Data Literacy Project (2021a) How to drive data literacy in the enterprise, https://thedataliteracyproject.org/resources (archived at https://perma.cc/FW23-63B3)

The Data Literacy Project (2021b) The Data Literacy Index, https://thedataliteracyproject.org/resources (archived at https://perma.cc/FW23-63B3)

The Data Literacy Project (2021c) The human impact of data literacy, https://thedataliteracyproject.org/resources (archived at https://perma.cc/FW23-63B3)

Chapter 8

Collins Dictionary (2021) Definition of "grass roots", https://www.collinsdictionary.com/us/dictionary/english/grass-roots (archived at https://perma.cc/3BNV-TPSS)

Dweck, C (2007) *Mindset: The New Psychology of Success*, Ballantine Books, New York

Goodreads (2021) Nelson Mandela quotes, https://www.goodreads.com/quotes/9041891-i-never-lose-i-either-win-or-learn (archived at https://perma.cc/XU7S-XW7B)

Grant, H and Rock, D (2016) Why diverse teams are smarter, *Harvard Business Review*, https://hbr.org/2016/11/why-diverse-teams-are-smarter (archived at https://perma.cc/WVQ9-7H8U)

Mailchimp (2021) Data bias is a people problem, https://mailchimp.com/resources/data-bias-causes-effects/ (archived at https://perma.cc/2C39-ZWDB)

Scott, SJ (2021) Fixed mindset vs. growth mindset: What REALLY matters for success, *Develop Good Habits*, https://www.developgoodhabits.com/fixed-mindset-vs-growth-mindset/ (archived at https://perma.cc/KF55-GVD3)

Smith, J (2020) Growth mindset vs fixed mindset: How what you think affects what you achieve, https://www.mindsethealth.com/matter/growth-vs-fixed-mindset (archived at https://perma.cc/9B3Z-7HKD)

The Data Lodge (2021) The Data Lodge: Your home for data literacy, https://www.thedatalodge.com (archived at https://perma.cc/K67Q-W9KB)

ThoughtSpot (2021) What is data fluency & why does it matter? https://www.thoughtspot.com/what-is-data-fluency-why-it-matters (archived at https://perma.cc/YU88-AWWG)

Chapter 9

Bornhofen, R (2021) If you can't explain it to a six year old, you don't understand it yourself, *Bizcatalyst360*, https://www.bizcatalyst360.com/if-you-cant-explain-it-to-a-six-year-old-you-dont-understand-it-yourself (archived at https://perma.cc/E5HP-SQFU)

Chapman, A (2020) How to identify your "desired business outcomes", *Totally Optimized Projects*, https://blog.totallyoptimizedprojects.com/top-thinking/how-to-identify-your-desired-business-outcomes (archived at https://perma.cc/2FTA-5P5F)

Haden, J (2021) 7 productivity rules Elon Musk says every effective leader should embrace, *Inc*, https://www.inc.com/jeff-haden/productivity-rules-elon-musk-says-every-effective-leader-should-embrace.html (archived at https://perma.cc/2QSK-QMSY)

MeetingKing (2015) How long should a meeting be? https://meetingking.com/how-long-should-a-meeting-be/ (archived at https://perma.cc/ZB43-JHNB)

Meyer-Cuno, D (2021) Is a vision statement important? *Forbes*, https://www.forbes.com/sites/forbesbooksauthors/2021/02/24/is-a-vision-statement-important/?sh=2d97c0ee3be7 (archived at https://perma.cc/6WGH-WW4U)

Chapter 10

Cote, C (2021) 5 principles of data ethics for business, *Harvard Business School Online*, https://online.hbs.edu/blog/post/data-ethics (archived at https://perma.cc/9C28-QTPC)

Coursera (2021) What is a data engineer? A guide to this in-demand career, https://www.coursera.org/articles/what-does-a-data-engineer-do-and-how-do-i-become-one (archived at https://perma.cc/MZL3-CCWA)

Dictionary.com (2021) Iteration, https://www.dictionary.com/browse/iteration (archived at https://perma.cc/AA85-P44K)

Hanegan, K (2019) Essential steps to making better data-informed decisions, *Qlik Blog*, https://www.qlik.com/blog/essential-steps-to-making-better-data-informed-decisions (archived at https://perma.cc/857Q-HT32)

Hanegan, K (2021) *Turning Data into Wisdom: How we collaborate with data to change ourselves, our organizations, and even the world*, self-published

Marr, B (2021) *Data Strategy: How to profit from a world of big data, analytics and artificial intelligence*, 2nd edition, Kogan Page, London

Oracle (2021) What is database management? https://www.oracle.com/database/what-is-data-management/ (archived at https://perma.cc/5UK2-LEA3)

Patruno, L (2021) What does it mean to deploy a machine learning model? *Kdnuggets*, https://www.kdnuggets.com/2020/02/deploy-machine-learning-model.html (archived at https://perma.cc/8JB9-5L7K)

Stedman, C and Vaughan, J (2020) What is data governance and why does it matter? *TechTarget*, https://searchdatamanagement.techtarget.com/definition/data-governance (archived at https://perma.cc/CNA8-L5UH)

Talend (2021) What is data integration? https://www.talend.com/resources/what-is-data-integration/ (archived at https://perma.cc/9H2B-YET6)

INDEX

The index is filed in alphabetical, word-by-word order. Acronyms are filed as presented and numbers as spelt out.

CPSIA information can be obtained
at www.ICGtesting.com
Printed in the USA
JSHW020046230722
28468JS00005B/33